THE
RUSSIAN
REVOLUTION

E. M. Halliday

HORIZON · NEW WORD CITY

Published by New Word City, Inc.

For more information about New Word City, visit our Web site at
NewWordCity.com

INTRODUCTION

The turbulent events that overtook Russia in 1917 are often called one of history's great turning points. In March of that year, a corrupt, outdated, beleaguered autocracy - the 300-year-old Romanov dynasty - was overthrown by an uprising of Russia's long-oppressed masses. During the next few months, Alexander Kerensky and other liberals in the provisional government attempted to adopt reforms. But the continuing hardships of World War I and the pressure of a radical minority, Vladimir Lenin's Bolsheviks, proved too much for them. In the relatively bloodless *coup d'état* of November 7, Lenin and his associates seized control of the state.

To understand and appreciate these historic events, one must look back to the nineteenth-century origins of Russian revolutionary thought, which can be traced to events that led to the abortive uprising of 1905 and the subsequent, short-lived reforms, and to the devastating war with Germany that caused an empire to stagger. The events were influenced by such personalities as the ineffectual Czar Nicholas and his domineering wife Alexandra, the sinister Grigori Efimovich Rasputin and his aristocratic murderer Prince Felix Yusupov, and - most importantly - the two men from nearly identical backgrounds who took such different paths, Kerensky and Lenin. These two, more than anyone else, guided the country in the days and years that followed the revolution.

In time, of course, the early attempts to liberalize the country gave way to dictatorship, repression, and cruelty. Even today, Lenin remains a hero to the Russian people, who have never fully known democracy or freedom. They have lived for centuries under government control in one form or another. The revolution of 1917, however, gave birth to communism, which went on to infect other countries and drive international conflicts for the remainder of the twentieth century.

1
THE UNEXPECTED
REVOLUTION

On March 9, 1917, a mounted Cossack winked at a striking workman as he galloped past him down a street in Russia's imperial capital, Petrograd – St. Petersburg until Czar Nicholas renamed it at the beginning of World War II. It may have been the most significant wink in modern history. It meant that Czar Nicholas II's best soldiers were going to abandon him down when the crucial moment came to suppress the mobs of rebellious workers who roamed the city on that Friday morning - the last Friday a czar would ever sit on the Russian throne.

The odd thing about the revolution that abruptly ended 300 years of rule by the House of Romanov was that no one planned it, and, therefore, no one expected it or foresaw just how it would unfold.

By the first weeks of 1917, it was already clear to almost everyone - except perhaps the czar and his wife - that the hundreds of thousands of factory workers in Petrograd were in a dangerously hostile mood. Labor strikes were increasing in number and intensity. For two and a half years, the nation had been at war with Germany and people were exhausted. Yet, a revolution to overthrow the government did not seem likely. The police of the capital city had been reinforced by a garrison of about 160,000 soldiers, all well-armed, and an elaborate plan had been designed to put down any revolt by striking laborers. As for the workers, despite their disgust with the war and their government and bitter discontent with the scarcity and cost of food and fuel, they did not consciously feel that the time was ripe for a violent overthrow of the regime. Yet active revolutionaries had infiltrated the manufacturing plants of Petrograd. It had always been assumed that such agitators would have planned the whole revolution step by step.

Many revolutionary leaders, however, were absent in March 1917. This was most notably true of the communists, or Social Democrats, as they were then called. Lenin, their guiding genius, was in Zurich, Switzerland, not optimistic about the chances of a revolution in Russia. Leon Trotsky, soon to become his chief lieutenant, was in New York City, where he helped edit a revolutionary newspaper. Stalin, the young man who one day would be the communist dictator, was in exile in Siberia. Although some other revolutionaries of distinction were present, they were, so to speak, absent in mind: They failed to gauge the mood of the people, and especially, the mood of the soldiers.

A good example was Alexander Kerensky, a brilliant young labor leader and member of the Russian legislative council, the Duma. At the end of February, he made bold speeches before that body suggesting that removal of Nicholas II - "by terrorist methods if there is no other way" - would solve the national problem; he was not thinking in terms of mass revolution. "I hope that Duma man Kedrinsky," wrote the czarina to the czar, getting the name wrong, "will be hung for his horrible speeches. It is necessary, and it will be an example."

But neither assassinating Czar Nicholas nor hanging men like Kerensky was the solution that history had in store.

On the cold Thursday morning of March 8, disturbances flared in the workers' sections of Petrograd. A number of women waiting in long queues in front of bakeries grew angry when they were told there was no more bread. That same morning, women employed at several Petrograd textile plants went out on strike. They were soon followed by thousands of men from the metal factories. The discontented workers began a demonstration, carrying banners that said, "We want bread." A crowd formed around them, and soon agitators were speaking on street corners, and people were shouting "down with the war" in addition to "we want bread." Police reserves were called out, but so far, there was little violence, although occasionally someone would pick up a chunk of ice from the snow-covered streets and hurl it at a passing officer.

In 1917, Russia was still using the Julian calendar, thirteen days behind the more prevalent Gregorian calendar. Thus, according to the old Russian calendar, the revolution began on February 23, and the overthrow of the czarist regime is sometimes referred to as the February revolution. For our purposes, we will use Gregorian dates.

By the morning of March 9, the streets of the city were jammed with crowds of strikers - estimated at close to 200,000, half of Petrograd's industrial labor force. It was apparent that a massive strike was developing, and the authorities nervously called out the Cossacks.

The Cossacks, on horseback and carrying their sabers, were the traditional instrument of the Russian monarchy for punishing troublesome citizens. They enjoyed special privileges in the army, and many a time, they had shown how fiercely and efficiently they could carry out the czar's orders. On March 9, 1917, they pranced their horses into the crowds as usual or broke into a galloping charge when ordered to do so by their officers. But the striking workers noticed a difference: The Cossacks exercised care with their sabers, left their firearms at their sides, and looked down on the upturned faces with a surprising lack of ferocity. Then came the wink that was to become famous. Shortly thereafter, the word flashed around that a Cossack patrol had driven off policemen who were beating up workers on a street corner. The next time a troop of Cossacks galloped through a crowd, they were greeted with hurrahs.

The military commander of Petrograd was baffled, but there seemed to be nothing to do but call out more soldiers. Most of the infantrymen, however, turned out to be even more inclined than the Cossacks to favor the people. They carried their bayoneted rifles at a harmless angle, and many of them started up friendly conversations with the strikers. Most of these soldiers were not professionals but peasants who had been forced from their villages to replace brothers and cousins killed or wounded in the war. They disliked military service and felt sympathy for a crowd of fellow citizens whose only demands seemed to be for bread and an end to the war.

By March 10, Petrograd was seething. Streetcars had stopped running, and thousands of shop clerks and students had joined the masses of striking laborers. The temperature was well below zero; great clouds of steam puffed from horses' nostrils and rose from the shouting and singing crowds.

The czar's ministers and the leading members of the Duma were startled and apprehensive as they watched the demonstrations of March 8 to March 11. They understood that a tremendous revolutionary force was erupting, and there seemed to be little possibility of controlling it. Agitated telegrams were dispatched to the czar, but his reactions were not helpful. On Saturday, March 10, he telegraphed the military commander at Petrograd: "I command you to suppress from tomorrow all disorders on the streets of the capital, which are impermissible at a time when the fatherland is carrying on a difficult war with Germany." The harassed commander prepared a proclamation to carry out the czar's order but could not find enough glue to post it on city streets.

By Monday, March 12, the tide of the revolution was at the full and there was no stopping it. The few companies of soldiers still under the command of the authorities were unreliable. When they were sent to form a new line of resistance against the rebellion, they simply dissolved into the crowds and their weapons became part of the revolutionary arsenal.

By this time, armored cars flying the red flag of socialism cruised the streets and the workers had taken over many machine guns. The people sensed victory was in sight; the excitement was keen. A journalist making his way across the turbulent city reported that cars and trucks kept going by "in which soldiers, workers, students, and young women, some wearing arm-bands, were sitting or standing. God knows where all these came from, where they were rushing to, or with what purpose. But all these passengers were extremely excited, shouting and waving their arms, scarcely aware of what they were doing." Everyone talked eagerly to everyone else, acquainted or not, trying to pick up information about the latest developments. Rumors flew, but there was one thing that all were sure of: The old order was giving way to the new.

Now the focus of the rebellion became the Tauride Palace, which held the Duma's meeting halls. The legislative body had been suspended by order of the czar, but some of the leaders favored ignoring the decree. On Monday morning, Duma members gathered at the Tauride to debate what their role ought to be. "I don't want to revolt," protested Duma president M. V. Rodzianko, and no doubt he expressed the feeling of the majority of his colleagues.

xxx

It was obvious to the Duma leaders that if any connections at all were going to be maintained with the old government, some kind of definite move would have to be made. Therefore, they hastily established the Temporary Committee of the Duma. The purpose of the committee, they announced, was to try to give some shape to the chaotic state of affairs in Petrograd, not to suppress the revolution (it was in any case too late for that), but to bring some order into its results.

Just a few hours later, another meeting was going on in the same Tauride Palace. There a kind of improvised staff of the unplanned revolution was belatedly set up. Some of the labor leaders, remembering the days of an earlier attempt at revolution in 1905, decided to reestablish a Soviet of Workers' Deputies. They named themselves as a temporary Executive Committee of the Soviet. (Soviet in Russian means council.) Delegates were to be elected immediately to the Soviet from all the local factories and also from the numerous military units that had now come over to the side of the revolution. The first meeting of the committee was to be held in the Tauride Palace that very night, March 12.

By late afternoon of that day, the delegates to the Soviet, plus large groups of their supporters, as well as the merely curious - a great mixed crowd of workers, soldiers, and students - were milling in and about the Tauride. The meeting began that evening, and after a long series of excited reports from soldier delegates - many of them still carrying their rifles - the delegates began to elect committees to deal with the most pressing problems of bringing order back to Petrograd.

So it was that from the beginning of the great Russian Revolution, two rival power centers were created. On the one hand was the Soviet of Workers' and Soldiers' Deputies (as it was now to be called), with its Executive Committee dominated by socialist labor leaders who insisted that Russia must become a republic. On the other hand, there was the Temporary Committee of the Duma, composed of liberal and moderately conservative politicians who were reluctant to place their hands on the torch of revolution. Many of them would have preferred to have the nation become a constitutional monarchy, still with a czar, but one whose dictatorial powers would be almost entirely taken away. They felt that such a government would be more likely to guarantee the property rights of the middle-class businessmen and upper-class landowners whom they represented.

There was one link between the two power centers - Alexander Kerensky, who was a member of both committees. His role, unavoidably, was going to be a highly important one, and he recognized it from the first. A man who was able to give the impression of great self-assurance in a crisis, he strode briskly through the halls of the Tauride Palace. He made dozens of speeches, ordered excited workers not to harm any of the members of the czar's Council of Ministers who had been rounded up and brought in as prisoners, and sent out detachments of soldiers to guard the railroad stations in case czarist troops were moved in from outside the city.

What of the czar? He had not yet given up his throne, yet without his knowing it, history already had passed him by. On the morning of Tuesday, March 13, a member of the Soviet Executive Committee, who, like many others, had spent the night curled up on his overcoat on the floor of the Tauride Palace, woke up to the grunts of a couple of soldiers who were poking at a big painting with their bayonets. It was a portrait of Nicholas II, and they were cutting the picture out of the frame to the accompaniment of uncomplimentary remarks.

Nicholas himself, on that morning, was on his private train, trying to get back to his palace at Tsarskoe Selo, a suburb of Petrograd. He wanted to be with his family, come what might. The railroad lines leading to Petrograd, however, had been taken over by rebels, and it soon became clear that they would interfere with the progress of the imperial train. Nicholas, therefore, turned aside and went to the headquarters of one of his generals, at a place called Pskov, arriving on the evening of Wednesday, March 14. The next day, he was informed that it was the opinion not only of the Temporary Committee of the Duma, but also of the generals in command of all the fighting fronts, that he must abdicate the throne.

The czar took this news calmly, almost as if emperors were asked to give up their crowns every day. Two members of the Duma arrived from Petrograd to receive Nicholas's signed abdication, and he listened with a look of patient boredom while they explained at length the necessity for this step. The only change he insisted on was that the throne should not go to his son (a boy of twelve in delicate health) but to his brother, the Grand Duke Michael.

The two Duma members left for Petrograd on the evening of Thursday, March 15, taking the abdication paper with them, and Nicholas wrote in his diary, before going to bed in his private car: "To save Russia and keep the army at the front, I decided upon this step . . . At 1 o'clock in the morning I left Pskov with heavy feelings; around me treason, cowardice, deceit."

Evidently, however, his heavy feelings were soon lightened by the reflection that the responsibilities of czardom, which he had always disliked, had now been lifted from his shoulders as if by a miracle. "I had a long and sound sleep," the diary entry for the next day reads. "Sunshine and frost . . . I read much of Julius Caesar." A week later, he was placed in captivity in his own home at Tsarskoe Selo, along with his beloved wife, Alexandra. Stifling her burning indignation at what had happened to her husband, the czarina busied herself with her children. All of them were sick with measles.

Back at the Tauride Palace in Petrograd, the events of the revolution had been plunging ahead. On March 15, the Temporary Committee of the Duma had announced, by agreement with the Petrograd Soviet, the formation of a provisional government (composed largely of the same group of men) that would rule the country until a national constituent assembly could meet. Such an assembly would have representatives from the entire country, and they would decide exactly what kind of nation Russia would now become. One thing was already certain: It would not be a monarchy, under either the Grand Duke Michael or anyone else. The Grand Duke, in fact, seeing how things were going, judiciously abdicated the throne without ever having occupied it.

Meanwhile, it was clear that the Soviet of Workers' and Soldiers' Deputies was going to act as a kind of unofficial congress or parliament; very little could be accomplished by the provisional government without its approval. For example, on March 14, the Soviet issued to the soldiers of the Petrograd garrison "Order No. 1," which soon became famous. It was interpreted as an order to democratize the army; soldiers were to have the same rights as other citizens except when actually performing military duties; there was to be no more off-duty saluting; all weapons were to be controlled by the enlisted men, not the officers. Furthermore, orders issued by the Duma military commission "should be carried out only in those cases where they do not contradict the orders of the Soviet of Workers' and Soldiers' Deputies." It has been said that Order No. 1 marked the start of a long struggle between the provisional government and the Soviet, a conflict that would finally be settled only by a second revolution, some eight months later - the Communist Revolution of November 1917.

For the time being, however, a kind of peace had descended on Russia. An enormous mountain of problems had to be immediately confronted, but at least the revolution that so many had dreamed of for so many decades, the revolution that would free Russia from czarism, had actually taken place, and with far less violence and bloodshed than anyone could have anticipated.

Fresh snow had fallen. Walking through the now nearly empty streets of Petrograd, a member of the Soviet Executive Committee was elated despite his fatigue. "I was walking," he wrote later, "through a free city of the new Russia . . . Where was czarism?

It was gone. It had crumbled away in an instant. Three centuries to build it up, and three days for it to vanish."

When Nicholas II was toppled from his throne by the Revolution in March 1917, he lost what in many ways was the most powerful monarchy in the world. Its strength came from sheer enormity: Russia's vast geographical area (almost as large as all of North America), its huge population (about 148 million in 1917), its abundant natural resources. And it was all held together for 300 years by the near total control of czarist rule. But the czars also used that power to enrich themselves and the nobility while trying to build Russia into one of the most important countries in the world.

In spite of rapid industrialization from the 1880s to the outbreak of World War I in 1914, Russia remained primarily an agricultural nation. More than 80 percent of its population was rural. Until 1861, the vast Russian farmlands were tilled by millions of serfs. These peasants "went with the land" and were actually the property of the noble landlords, like cattle or sheep. The serfs, of course, had no voice in how the great empire was run. As long as the czar could count on the loyal support of his nobles, he was a true autocrat with absolute authority. The laws of the realm were what he wanted them to be.

On top of that, however, the Russian government

itself owned nearly half the peasants. Huge tracts of land were farmed for the benefit of the Russian state and the czar's private treasury. The government was also in charge of extensive enterprises that in the United States and Western Europe would have been left largely in private hands. It owned and operated many industrial plants, as well as the railroads and all other communications; it supported and controlled the Russian Orthodox Church, the official state church, and all schools and universities; it also censored all publications. The czar commanded an enormous army and navy, adding to his power. It helped, too, that the royal ruler had the love and support of many of the middle and lower classes, who were used to having the state hover over their lives.

Much of Russian history is heavy with the great, sullen masses of underprivileged peasants whose frustrated human desires might at some time break out into the open. From time to time there actually were rebellions, nearly 2,000 in all, touched off when the serfs were aroused by intolerable conditions to lash out against their masters and the czar in hope of better treatment. Oddly, the leaders of such rebellions often became romantic figures even in the eyes of the aristocrats, as if the idea of a violent blow for freedom appealed to the Russian spirit regardless of one's particular social status.

It was not until the early nineteenth century, however, that there was a revolt based on any plan of reforming the Russian government. Significantly, it was organized by a group of young nobles, rather than by anyone from the underprivileged classes. In December 1825, the succession of Czar Nicholas I to the throne was resisted by some young army officers and intellectuals. The movement was quickly crushed: Nicholas had five of the conspirators executed and many others exiled in Siberia. But the Decembrists, as they were called, were fondly remembered by Russians who longed for a freer society.

Among the aims of the Decembrists had been the abolition of serfdom and the setting up of a constitutional government. For nearly a century, educated Russians - which meant, largely, the nobility - would be divided among those who supported the czar as an all-powerful dictator; those who sought moderate reform that would make the czar a constitutional monarch like the king of England; and those who wished to overthrow the government altogether.

The Russian countryside was dominated by the manor houses of the nobility and landed gentry. Society was divided into classes: bureaucrats and professionals, the judges, doctors, teachers; next the priests and shopkeepers, artisans, servants; and at the bottom, the millions of serfs, little more than slaves, on whose backs the autocracy depended.

Alexander II, the son of Nicholas I, aroused much hope among his people, for he decreed the emancipation of the serfs in 1861, six years after he came to the throne. Yet, as it worked out, few of the liberated peasants were much better off afterward than they had been before. They no longer were the property of the landlords, but the amount of land they were allotted was not enough to support their families. This was partly because of the steady growth of Russia's peasant population, partly because of their primitive, inefficient farming methods, and partly because of complicated legal requirements on how their land was to be held. The peasant question, as it was called, was not solved by emancipation.

Besides bringing an end to serfdom, Alexander took other steps toward modernizing the heavy and backward social structure of his country. A system of local self-government was instituted - the *zemstvos*, or county councils, whose members were elected by the people. Other reforms soon followed. Schools, hospitals, and roads were improved and rapidly increased in number; newer methods of agriculture were introduced; censorship of newspapers and books was eased somewhat; trial by jury was established to give accused persons a greater chance for justice. The reforms held the promise of a new, freer era. One observer at the time noted, "It seems as if out of a dark dungeon we were emerging, if not into God's light, at least into an anteroom where we could sense refreshing air." But the national government continued to play a big role in Russian society, in some respects more so than before.

Alexander lived to regret many of the reforms. It must have seemed to him that people were ungrateful. Revolutionary groups, instead of fading away, were stimulated by the gains already made to demand more radical changes. Among the most active and numerous of the reformers were the Narodniks (literally, populists), most of them students, who wished to turn the government over to the people in a form of socialism. They came to idealize the peasant and make him the focus of all their reform efforts.

In a movement of the early 1870s, Narodniks went to the people almost like missionaries, hoping to arouse the peasants to a revolution that would overthrow the czarist autocracy. Most peasants, however, were not ready for such a message and suspiciously regarded the Narodniks as troublesome outsiders. The program was not a success.

In desperation, some of the Narodniks formed a secret organization called The People's Will, with cells that met regularly to plan acts of terror. Many such plans were boldly carried out: Trains were dynamited, officials assassinated, government buildings bombed. There were several unsuccessful attempts on the czar's life. Then, in March 1881, as Alexander rode through St. Petersburg, a member of The People's Will tossed a bomb at his coach. Two Cossack guards fell to the ground, and the czar leaped out to help them, meeting a second explosion. He died an hour and a half later from his wounds. Five young members of The People's Will, including Sophie Perovskaya, the daughter of a prominent government official, were hanged for the assassination.

Alexander II, only a few hours before his sudden death, had approved a plan for a consultative council that would have given the public some voice in national affairs. The shock of the assassination brought an end to that. His son, Alexander III, turned his attention instead to expanding the network of his secret police in order to counteract further terrorism. His thirteen-year reign was an almost uninterrupted series of repressions, even though it was a period of great national progress for Russia in terms of industrial development and railroad building. One important result was that, over time, large numbers of people moved from agriculture to factory work.

A plot to kill Alexander III was thwarted in 1887, and one of the executed leaders was Alexander Ulyanov. This young revolutionary had a seventeen-year-old brother named Vladimir Ilyich. He was a bright and studious boy with an intense personality, and he was soon to become a political agitator himself. Like most Russian revolutionaries of the far left, young Ulyanov chose an alias, one that would later become famous in the Russian Revolution: Lenin.

Vladimir Ilyich Ulyanov grew up in a middle-class family. His father was in charge of local schools, and the number of elementary schools in their province increased from 20 to 434 under his administration. The young Ulyanov was an excellent student and finished high school with a glowing recommendation from his headmaster: "Very gifted student, always neat and assiduous, Ulyanov was always first in all his subjects." The glowing recommendation went on at length, then ended with this observation: "a somewhat excessive tendency to isolation and reserve, a tendency to avoid contact with acquaintances and even with the very best of his school fellows outside of school hours." The year before his last year of high school, Lenin's father died in front of him of a massive stroke. Only a year later, his older brother was hanged for the assassination attempt. Though the brothers were not close, Lenin would also be radicalized. But he didn't want to overthrow one man; he wanted to overthrow the entire system.

Lenin went on to study law at home, cramming four years of study into one. When he sat for the law exam, he emerged again as first in his class. During this time, he encountered the work of Karl Marx and became an avid student of Marx's communist idealism. Marx believed the revolution, the movement to change everything, would happen in the cities, so Lenin moved to St. Petersburg. He was twenty-three and joined a Marxist study group just one year before Czar Nicholas would take the throne.

Following a trip to Europe, where he met with other radicals, Lenin returned to Russia and started organizing strikes. He was arrested and exiled to Siberia for three years. The exile was not a great hardship, requiring only that he live in a prescribed area. The three years, spent largely in studying radical philosophy and writing, were among the happiest in his life. It was there, in the village of Shushkenkoe on the Shush River, that he wrote his own manifesto, *The Development of Capitalism in Russia*. His fiancée, Nadezhda "Nadya" Krupskaya, a schoolteacher he had met in St. Petersburg, who had also been arrested, joined him in Siberia, and he kept up a flowing correspondence with his Marxist friends. So it was not the hard life many imagine.

By now, he had acquired a reputation as a revolutionary. When his term was up, he returned briefly to St. Petersburg before exiling himself to Europe, leaving his now-wife Krupskaya in Siberia to serve out the rest of her term. In Europe, he became part of the underground and an editor and writer for the radical magazine *Iskra*, the *Spark*. He then took up the pen name Lenin, which would live on long after his death.

Lenin's pamphlet, *What Is To Be Done?*, which he had written in exile, became gospel for the Social Democrats, as they now called themselves. He and Krupskaya, who had completed her sentence, moved to London, which had become headquarters for Russian exiles. Lenin grew in reputation and leadership, developing a wide following both among the exiles and the growing revolutionary movement at home. He soon broke with another leader, Georgi Plekhanov, largely over how the group should be organized. Lenin prevailed, and his group, took the name Bolsheviks, which means majority. The losers were the Mensheviks, Russian for minority.

Quite unexpectedly, Alexander III died of a bronchial infection in 1894. Nicholas II, the next czar - and destined to be the last - possessed a character very different from that of his father. Both of them were handsome and well built, but there the resemblance ended. The father, Alexander III, had exactly the temperament of an autocrat: He was imperious in manner, sure of his feelings and ideas, quick to make hard and fast decisions, merciless toward anyone who crossed his will. Nearly everything he said was in the form of a command, and his commands were obeyed without question.

Nicholas - perhaps because he spent his boyhood in the shadow of this overwhelming father - was by contrast polite, quiet, often unsure of his opinion and likely to change it abruptly under pressure. He found disagreement of any kind unpleasant and always tried to avoid arguments. He charmed everyone. "A spirit of good will radiated brightly from him," said one of his government ministers, one who, in fact, was not fond of him. Yet this charm could be deceptive; for example, he would sometimes dismiss an astonished official the morning after having entertained him in the imperial palace with every show of affection.

The truth is that Nicholas was not cut out to be an autocratic ruler. He might have made a good king of England, like his first cousin George V, whom he so much resembled. A strong prime minister and an independent parliament were the sort of guides he needed. But in Russia, where everything depended on the decision of the emperor, he was fated to be a failure. He seemed to sense this himself. Although as czar he dutifully attended to his obligations, he lived for the hours when he could be away from official functions altogether, to play with his children, take tea with his wife, or go outdoors for one of the many sports he enjoyed, such as swimming or hunting.

As historical luck would have it, this amiable individual fell in love, when still very young, with a girl whose personality was destined to make his weaknesses count more rather than less. Princess Alix of Hesse-Darmstadt was a German by birth, but she had been brought up from the age of six by her grandmother, Queen Victoria of England. As might have been expected, her notions of etiquette, of morality, and of religion were Victorian to the highest degree - that is to say, rigid and narrow, but rooted in very strong convictions. The education her tutors gave her was sketchy on the side of information and reasoning; any high school graduate today understands a good deal more about the world than this elegant princess did when, as a seventeen-year-old, she spent six weeks in St. Petersburg and the twenty-one-year-old Nicholas fell in love with her.

Alix was a pretty girl, but to most members of the Russian court and St. Petersburg society, her charm was a secret that only Nicholas grasped. Despite a stubborn will, she was outwardly shy; besides, at first, she spoke no Russian. (She and Nicholas carried on their courtship in English and it was to be the language of their intimate life together.) Then there was the obstacle of her religion; she had been raised in the Church of England, and the idea of converting to the strange rites of the Russian Orthodox faith at first repelled her.

Once she had made the decision, however, Alix embraced her new creed with fervent enthusiasm. She seemed to feel that total devotion to the Russian form of Christianity would make up for her German birth, her English upbringing, and her natural awkwardness with everything else that was Russian. Besides, according to the Orthodox Church, the czar was directly anointed by God as the leader of his people. This anointed man became her own beloved husband, and before long the father of her children, and her religious feelings tended to get tangled up with her family loyalty.

Nicholas's marriage to Alix came a few weeks after his father's death in 1894. His coronation, for which elaborate preparations were necessary, had to wait until May 1896. This great event at Russia's old capital, Moscow, was marked by two accidents that must have struck millions of Russians as bad omens; they certainly so struck the czarina, for she proved early to be a very superstitious woman.

During the coronation ceremony, a St. Andrew's Cross that Nicholas was wearing fell unaccountably to the floor. A few hours later, through unbelievable mismanagement on the part of police authorities, there was a horrible panic in a field tightly crowded with peasants who had come to Moscow to see the new czar. It was customary on such an occasion to distribute small presents to the poor, and somehow the rumor started that there were not enough gifts to go around. The crowd surged forward, some wooden covers over several deep ditches gave way, and an estimated 2,000 were crushed to death or suffocated in the trample. Whether because he failed to understand what had happened or because of his tendency to look the other way from anything unpleasant, the newly crowned czar made matters worse by proceeding calmly to the French ambassador's ball, with lavish food, wine, music, and dancing. People began talking of the czar's birth on the feast of St. Job as a further omen that he too would be beset with troubles sent from God.

Nicholas revered his father's memory, and this gave rise to a fatal paradox. Unsuited for absolute monarchy, he nevertheless announced that nothing was going to change: "I shall maintain the principle of autocracy just as firmly and unflinchingly as it was preserved by my unforgettable dead father." In this attitude, he was enthusiastically supported by his young wife; in fact, right from the start, Alix - or Alexandra, as she was now called - felt that Nicholas was inclined to be too unaggressive. Even before they were married, she had written him the first of what were to be many messages urging him to take a stronger stand: "Show your own mind and don't let others forget who you are."

All that was needed to make the reign of Nicholas II just as undemocratic and reactionary as his father's were government ministers who leaned the same way, and during his early years as czar, there was no lack of these. Liberals at the universities, reformers attempting to work at the local level through the *zemstvos*, journalists who tried to advance new social ideas in their newspapers, all were systematically repressed and persecuted, while the police ferreted out revolutionaries of every description. Minority groups, too, such as the Poles, the Finns, and the Jews, were treated with cruel injustice.

There were 5 million Jews in Russia, mostly in western Russia. They were incorporated into the empire when eastern Poland became part of the Russian state. Anti-Semitism grew, and they were subject to Russification and religious persecution. In December 1791, an area called the Pale of Settlement was created where Jews were required to live. Alexander I and Nicholas I tried to integrate the Jews, encouraging them to become Christian, but without much success. The assassination of Alexander II and the terrorism of the time were blamed on Jews. Beginning in April 1881, there were more than 200 pogroms with deaths in the thousands and destruction of property.

Nicholas II permitted one of the worst massacres of Jews, at the city of Kishinev in 1903, before the Nazi atrocities of World War II. It was his naive belief that nine-tenths of political agitators and revolutionaries were Jews, whereas, in fact, nearly all of his major critics were Christian, many of them noblemen.

But suppression breeds opposition, and a wide variety of groups opposed to the Russian autocracy continued to meet and talk and think and plan ways of reaching out toward greater freedom. There were two basic groups: the true revolutionaries, who felt that only a more or less violent overthrow of the existing regime could save Russia; and the liberals, who felt that if the czar would grant certain fundamental reforms, the nation could gradually work its way toward constitutional liberty without bloodshed.

Feeling the need for tighter organization, the revolutionaries formed parties, not political parties in the usual sense, but societies whose aim was to bring about a revolution by arousing the people. The largest of these organizations was that of the Socialist Revolutionaries, or SRs, as they were often called. This party was an outgrowth of The People's Will of the earlier period, and its program called for, above everything else, turning over all land to the peasants who worked it. The power of the czar and indeed the czar himself would be eliminated in a relatively quiet revolution and replaced by a more enlightened government.

The Social Democrats, or SDs, whose name sounded more peaceful, were actually a much more radical group. These men followed the teachings of German thinker Karl Marx. In his 1867 book, *Das Kapital*, Marx had predicted a completely new social structure in which all natural resources, and everything else that could be used to produce goods of any kind, would belong to the government in the name of the people. This new system would be called communism. It would come, Marx said, after a total revolution by the proletariat - the working class. Under the old system, capitalism, the workers owned little beyond the clothes on their backs, even though their labor produced the world's wealth.

The SDs, or Russian Marxists, were such a clear threat to the existing society that the czar's police made it impossible for their leaders to stay in Russia. Plekhanov, the father of the movement, set up his headquarters in Switzerland.

By 1903, it was already clear that Lenin was determined to lead the Russian Marxists the way a general leads an army. Rather short and stocky, with a domelike bald head, he was personally not very impressive until he began to speak. Then the enormous intensity of the man would begin to show in his iron will and ambitious drive. Lenin argued constantly and vehemently for the violent overthrow of the czar and the capitalist class, so that a "dictatorship of the proletariat" could be established to pave the way to true communism.

He differed from Marx: He believed a small, highly centralized party of revolutionaries would lead the people while Marx advocated for a majority of the people to seize power. "There is no other man who is absorbed by the revolution twenty-four hours a day," a fellow conspirator wrote of Lenin, "who has no other thoughts but the thought of revolution, and who, even when he sleeps, dreams of nothing but the revolution."

Typically, Lenin scorned SDs who wanted to take a more gradual course toward revolution, and his insistence brought about a split in the party. At a series of argumentative meetings, which began in Brussels and ended in London in 1903, Lenin got more than half of his forty-two fellow conspirators to vote for his revolutionary program, from that moment on known as the Bolsheviks.

In Russia, the real majority of social reformers were neither SRs nor SDs but moderate liberals who had not yet organized into parties. They met in secret meetings all over Russia to discuss what might be done. And when they did, political arrests increased, as many as 6,000 in 1903. Most of the liberals had studied British constitutional history, admired the parliamentary system, and hoped that the czar might allow a similar system to be set up in Russia. They were about to have better luck in that direction than could reasonably have been expected at the turn of the century.

In 1904, Nicholas II managed to get his nation embroiled in a war with Japan that would shake his autocracy to its foundations.

2
WAR AND REBELLION

One day early in his reign, Nicholas II was riding in his royal carriage with Kaiser Wilhelm of Germany. Sixteen years later, these two monarchs were to face each other in a long and devastating war, but now they were on polite if not friendly terms. Wilhelm, a first cousin of Alexandra's, and distantly related to Nicholas, took the czar in hand and for ten years influenced him on foreign policy. Wilhelm had ambitions to expand Germany's overseas holdings and asked the czar if he would object to a German seizure of the Chinese port of Kiaochow. Nicholas said he would not mind, and afterward justified his agreement on the ground that the kaiser was his guest and he did not wish to be discourteous to him. When Germany did, indeed, take over Kiaochow, Nicholas made a step in the same direction by obtaining a lease of Port Arthur, another strategic port on China's Yellow Sea.

When governments are in trouble at home, it is often thought to be a good device to distract the people by getting involved in some international adventure. In 1904, Nicholas was persuaded to take this step by his reactionary ministers, who thought that "a small victorious war" would cure some of the great discontent that was disturbing Russia. Perhaps it might even stave off a revolution.

Korea looked like a good place to start trouble, and Russia made a gesture toward occupying that country, much to the anger of the Japanese, who had the same idea. The result was a relatively small but far from victorious war with Japan, for right from the start, the Japanese army and navy got the jump on the Russians. They landed troops in Korea and blockaded Port Arthur. Then Japanese divisions moved into Manchuria to drive back the troops the czar had sent to the Pacific on the Trans-Siberian Railroad.

Over several months, Russia suffered heavy losses. Instead of distracting the Russian people, the unsuccessful war made them angrier with their government. In January 1905, the Japanese staged a surprise attack on Port Arthur, which fell to the enemy; in May, a Russian fleet of antiquated warships, which had laboriously steamed 12,000 miles to do battle with the Japanese navy, was almost entirely destroyed in the Sea of Japan.

The Russians' savage defeat at the hands of the Japanese navy had a dramatic impact on military thinking in Europe and the United States. The prospect of losing a war in one afternoon was too much. There would be no more divided battle fleets. The Japanese, in one afternoon's encounter at sea, had frightened the greatest navies in the world.

Defeated in war, the Russians made gains against the Japanese during the peace conference hosted by U.S. President Theodore Roosevelt. Czar Nicholas's emissary criticized the Japanese in the U.S. press, creating ill will toward them, while developing good feelings toward the Russians by being especially nice to everyone he met in America. In the end, the Japanese made concessions at the bargaining table.

The kaiser was not entirely displeased by the Russian defeat in Japan. His friend the czar was now less of a threat and even more amenable to his manipulations, primarily to break the French-Russian alliance. He influenced Nicholas into signing an agreement between their two countries against France. The treaty caused great alarm in both Russia and Germany, and Nicholas was persuaded by his ministers to reject it. This marked the end of the personal friendship between the kaiser and the czar, but it came late. Nicholas had been soundly defeated in a war he entered at the kaiser's urging, and now he faced revolution at home.

Meanwhile, in the late fall of 1904, a convention of representatives from the *zemstvos* had respectfully but unanimously asked the czar for national reforms. First they requested a guarantee of such civil liberties as freedom of the press, freedom from arbitrary arrest, and freedom of assembly. They also asked for a representative body, a kind of parliament or congress, to act with the czar in either a consultative or legislative capacity. This request was enthusiastically supported by a large number of professional societies, such as those of lawyers, doctors, engineers, and journalists. It became clear that the better-educated classes of Russians were going to insist on moving the country toward democracy.

One group in the national movement of protest was composed of the factory workers - Lenin's proletariat - who now made up a considerable part of the working population, especially in and around St. Petersburg. The police had been well aware that the SDs were energetically propagandizing this important group. To counter the Marxist influence, they invented a workers' movement that they would control. Secretly they enlisted a priest, Father Georgiy Gapon, whose job was to pretend to lead the workers in a socialist organization. It was called the Assembly of Russian Workingmen, and the goal was to get the workers to channel their grievance away from the monarchy and toward their employers. This, the police hoped, would serve to let off steam and at the same time keep them in close touch with the real revolutionary activities of the proletariat.

Father Gapon, however, was more genuinely concerned with the workers' welfare than the police realized. He believed he could assist them in a noble cause to better their conditions without violence. In early 1905, the humiliating defeat against the Japanese sent a wave of protest through St. Petersburg as thousands of workers went on strike. Father Gapon, now compelled to lead the workers, went from meeting to meeting extolling them to join with him in petitioning the czar with their demands: a national assembly, universal suffrage, a minimum wage and eight-hour workday, separation of church and state, amnesty for all political prisoners. It was quite a list, and Father Gapon imagined leading the workers to the palace, placing the petition in Nicholas's hands, and experiencing a great victory. To dramatize their demands, Father Gapon organized a giant march on the Winter Palace in St. Petersburg on Sunday, January 22, 1905. There was to be no violence: The workers would simply carry religious banners, sing patriotic songs, and show the government their unanimous desire for a more liberal society.

The crowds - some 200,000 strong - moved slowly and peacefully toward the palace on that winter Sunday morning. The czar's guards and the police grew uneasy, and with little warning, they began to shoot. By official estimates, about 200 demonstrators were wounded and 150 killed. The actual numbers likely were much higher. Father Gapon vanished. The tragedy became known as Bloody Sunday. When word reached Great Britain, the czar was attacked as a "common murderer" and "blood-stained creature." From his hiding place, Father Gapon referred to Nicholas as the "soul-murderer of the Russian Empire." He was now a full-fledged revolutionary; however, fellow revolutionaries and workers no longer trusted him because of his police association. They sentenced him to death; the following year he was found hanged.

When news of the Bloody Sunday massacre spread across Russia, it raised an enormous outcry. Factory strikes broke out like a rash; police and government officials were murdered in scores of towns and villages.

Violence spread all over Russia. Nicholas wrote, "It makes me sick to read the news. Strikes in schools and factories, murdered policemen, Cossacks, riots. The ministers instead of acting with quick decision, only assemble in council like a lot of frightened hens."

But then the czar made one of those sudden switches that were a clue to his weak and wavering personality. Under pressure from some of his advisors, he offered the nation what until that moment Russian reformers had only dreamed of: a representative national assembly, to be known as the Imperial Duma. (Duma is derived from the Russian word meaning to think; used as a noun, it suggests a body of men who would consider and advise on important governmental problems.)

All over Russia, there was tremendous excitement at this development, and various groups began to form political parties to get ready for the expected elections and to suggest to the government what the functions of the Duma ought to be. In July 1905, a congress of representatives from the *zemstvos* and town councils issued a statement expressing the fervent hope of the Russian people that "a new order of things" could at last be achieved, and "without convulsions, without bloodshed, without thousands of unnecessary victims."

But when the government announced its precise plans for the Duma in August, there was deep disappointment. The electorate was mainly limited to the nobility, urban bourgeoisie, landed gentry, and peasants acting through the *zemstvos*. Important sections of the populace, including workers and minorities, such as Jews, were excluded. Instead of being a true legislature that could make binding laws, the new body would be just advisory. The czar and his ministers could take the Duma's advice or leave it.

What followed was one of the most astonishing strikes in modern times. Far from being limited to one industry, it spread spontaneously from the railroads to every type of factory; from there to power plants, stores, banks, restaurants, newspapers, hospitals. Everything shut down as if someone had pulled a gigantic lever. The Russian Empire was paralyzed. In St. Petersburg, in Moscow, in all the big cities, excited crowds roamed the streets waving red flags and listening to street-corner orators demanding democracy for Russia.

This was a showdown and the czar's ministers knew it. Count Sergei Witte, his leading advisor, who had just concluded the peace treaty with Japan in which Russia came off remarkably well, told the czar that only two paths were open. Either Russia must be granted a Duma empowered to make genuine laws, or a military dictatorship must be set up to avoid total revolution. The czar considered making his second cousin, the Grand Duke Nicholas Nikolayevich, military dictator, but that soldier and patriot announced he would shoot himself unless the czar allowed a legislative Duma. "It is necessary for the good of Russia," he said, "and of all of us." Very grudgingly, the czar agreed to "this terrible decision," as he called it in a letter to his mother.

Thus Russia became a constitutional monarchy, at least in theory. The Imperial Manifesto of October 30, 1905, provided for fundamental civil liberties and promised to expand the electorate. Moreover, the Duma's approval was to be required for all Russian laws. Everywhere gratitude and hope prevailed. The liberals, feeling that their day had finally come, proceeded openly to organize a party called the Kadets (after the Russian initials, KD, of their official name, Constitutional Democrats). The moderate conservatives also formed a party, the Octobrists, indicating their satisfaction with the October Manifesto. The extreme conservatives were appalled. They reacted by setting off (with police encouragement) a new series of bloody pogroms against the Jews, who were accused of being responsible for the revolutionary flames now beginning to lick at the structure of Russian society.

As for the Socialist Revolutionaries and Social Democrats, they hardly knew what to do. Many doubted Nicholas's sincerity in issuing the Manifesto. Others feared that the great concession made by the government would let the pressure out of the revolutionary movement like air out of a pricked balloon. The SRs had been agitating strenuously among the peasants, and late in 1905, catching the revolutionary spirit of the rest of the country, thousands of peasants rebelled against their landlords, burning down manor houses and expelling their former masters.

The SDs, for their part, refused to accept the October Manifesto, denouncing it in the pages of a new newspaper called *Izvestia* (News), the first issue of which came out the very day of the October 17 proclamation. Under the leadership of the Mensheviks - and especially of a dynamic young man named Leon Trotsky - they formed in St. Petersburg a Soviet, which became the model for similar groups in other cities. The basis for representation was one deputy for every 1,000 workers.

The St. Petersburg Soviet tried to continue the general strike with demands for an eight-hour workday; but now the mass of the people were not behind them. The leaders of the Soviet were arrested in December 1905, while a brief outbreak of violence in Moscow was soon put down by government troops.

The revolution of 1905 was petering out. Elections were indeed held for the Duma, and the results put the moderately liberal Kadets into the largest number of seats. Even they were far too liberal for the czar, and from the start, Duma and government faced each other like boxers in a ring.

At this moment in history, a great opportunity was open to Russia. The country might have evolved gradually toward a system of representative government of a Western European type, with respect for individual rights, rather than retain as it did the state-oriented system favoring autocracy. The *principle* of representative government had been granted. Economically, the nation was beginning to make huge strides, for Russia's natural resources were second to none; it had plenty of manpower, and Western technology was being very successfully applied to its industries. In some ways, the fact that Russia had been backward was a peculiar advantage; for instance, the big-business, mass-production super-factory, which was still a new thing even in the United States, was installed almost from the start in certain Russian industries - metal production was one - without the slow steps of growth that had been necessary elsewhere.

Unhappily, the great opportunity was missed. On one side, the Duma members spent their energies either squabbling among themselves about political differences or making extreme, idealistic demands on the government that obviously would not be granted. On the other side, the czar and his leading ministers, having quelled the revolution of 1905 by permitting the Duma to come into existence, began right away to curtail its powers and block its attempts to take an active part in the government of the Russian Empire. Anything dealing with foreign policy, foreign loans, or the army and navy was declared outside the Duma's jurisdiction.

Limited to domestic and civil affairs, the Duma then proposed to the government a new distribution of land to the peasants. Nicholas sent I. L. Goremykin, his aged prime minister, to scold the Duma for this "inadmissible" suggestion. The Duma then passed a resolution censuring the government, that is, the czar's Council of Ministers. Nicholas was furious, and on July 21, 1906, he dissolved the Duma by imperial decree. The council for which such hopes were held had been in session for only a little over two months.

At this, some 200 liberals in the Duma rushed across the border into nearby Finland, where they met under the trees in a forest, and issued a statement urging resistance to the czar's government. The only important result was that they were blacklisted, so that when a new Duma was elected in March 1907, the rebels were ineligible. Consequently, the Second Duma had fewer distinguished liberals among its membership and was a more conservative group.

In the meantime, a new prime minister, P. A. Stolypin, had taken advantage of the temporary absence of the Duma to try to calm the unsettled condition of the country in two rather contradictory ways. With his right hand, so to speak, he had the SR and SD terrorists tried by military courts and shot in large numbers; with his left, he rapidly pushed through reform measures that gave the Russian peasants more personal liberty than they had ever had before. For example, after the emancipation of the serfs, the land each peasant family was entitled to work for its own needs was merely a number of narrow strips among many, all belonging to the village in common, the so-called commune system. Stolypin's new law gave the head of a peasant family individual property rights for the first time, even though the process of bringing the law into effect proved to be painfully slow.

From the shelter of the Imperial Palace at Tsarskoe Selo, Nicholas and Alexandra watched the operation of the First and Second Dumas with dismay. Both of them felt that the very idea of a representative assembly violated the sacred heritage of the Russian autocracy, and as soon as Nicholas found an excuse, he dissolved the Second Duma just as eagerly as he had the First. This time, the excuse was a charge that the SD members of the Duma were involved in a plot to get the army to mutiny. The plot turned out later to be a police fake, but it was a good enough reason for the czar, and he sent the Second Duma to their homes after a session that had lasted about three months.

Although the people of Russia had profited very little so far from their evolving parliamentary system, they were by no means willing to give it up, and the czar's ministers realized that. The revolutionary excitement of 1905 had been replaced by a sullen discontent that expressed itself in various subtle but still unmistakable ways. The most popular Russian song right after the dissolution of the Second Duma, for instance, was written by Maxim Gorky, the famous revolutionary novelist and playwright. It was called "At the Bottom."

So, in 1907, a third Duma was elected, only under a new electoral law rigged in such a way that most members would be heavily biased in favor of the wealthy, conservative class, the strongest supporters of the Russian autocracy. Nevertheless, a majority of the newly elected representatives were intelligent, well-educated men who saw that if Russia were to avoid a disastrous revolution, the process of reform must not be cut off completely. Even this Duma, therefore, seemed hardly likely to please Nicholas and Alexandra, who nervously felt they had created a monster that would destroy them if it were not kept in a tightly locked cage.

Their fears were somewhat reduced by the fact that in Stolypin, they had a very able and hard-working prime minister. His efforts were matched in the Duma by those of Alexander Guchkov, a colorful soldier of fortune who had traveled widely and fought against England in the Boer War in South Africa. Guchkov was the chief of the Octobrists, the moderate conservatives who now dominated the Duma despite the rigging of the electoral law. He and Stolypin led the nation to some important accomplishments. Several millions of peasants were able to exchange the separated strips of land allotted to them by the village commune for single farms that truly belonged to them. Individual enterprise came into play, and farm production began to rise sharply.

Manufacturing and railroad building, too, made progress at a good pace, so that one of the closest observers of the Russian scene, the British scholar Sir Bernard Pares, remarked: "There can be no doubt that economically the seven years from 1907 to 1914 were, so far, the most prosperous period in Russian history." Besides great economic advances, the public school system was being greatly expanded during these years, and the army and navy were being overhauled. It can be seen that even though sovereign and Duma had failed to make the most of the chance offered by the revolution of 1905, the colossal and backward Russian nation was finally beginning to move forward at an encouraging rate.

But the hopeful season was due for some very bad weather. Stolypin, who made many enemies because of his brusque and forthright approach to governmental problems, was fatally wounded during a theatrical performance in September 1911. The czar, who was also in the audience, wrote his mother an eyewitness account of the incident, including the comment: "People were trying to lynch the assassin. I am sorry to say the police rescued him from the crowd." As for Czarina

Alexandra, she was not sorry to see Stolypin go. She was incapable of understanding that his strong leadership had temporarily bolstered the shaky foundation of her husband's throne. The stubborn czarina firmly warned the next prime minister, Count Vladimir Kokovtsev, that he must not, like Stolypin, "overshadow his sovereign."

In actuality, after Stolypin's death, Nicholas was beginning to fall under the shadow not of his prime minister but of a strange intruder named Rasputin, who had no official position yet wielded much power.

3
THE STRANGE
INFLUENCE OF RASPUTIN

Although the married life of Nicholas II and Alexandra has often been described as a model of domestic bliss, there was one shadow that hung constantly over their household. After producing four pretty daughters, the czarina had finally given birth to a male child in 1904. But the joy that greeted the arrival of the boy, who presumably would someday be czar, was soon checked. It was discovered that he had inherited from his mother a disease called hemophilia. This affliction causes uncontrolled bleeding at the slightest cut or bruise and can be fatal. The royal family lived in dread that they would lose their golden boy. The czarina exhausted herself between keeping long vigils over her son and praying for a miracle that might save him.

This was the situation when Rasputin arrived on the scene, having been introduced to the czar and czarina by a grand duchess who had heard about his acts of faith healing. The year was 1905, and for some time, this bearded peasant from Siberia had been wandering around Russia as a *starets*, or elder - a kind of vagrant pilgrim and self-appointed man of God.

Little was known about Rasputin, but in his part of Siberia, he already had a wide and curious reputation. He came from the village of Pokrovskoe, where he had been born about 1871, the son of a relatively well-to-do peasant. He had a dual reputation almost from the beginning. He was the most lecherous young man in town, yet he early showed gifts of and prophetic powers, which cast a glow of religious sanctity about him. It was said he could heal with a glance and could predict the weather for farmers months ahead. As he grew older, he would disappear from home for long intervals. Some said he was fasting and doing penance at monasteries, others that he had joined a secret group known as the *Khlysts*, who held frenzied rites in torch lit forest glades. There seems to be evidence that both sides of the story were partly true. He was readily accepted in the Russian tradition of wandering ascetics thought to be holy men. In many villages, they were seen as holier than local priests. Fyodor Dostoyevsky wrote about the *starets* in *The Brothers Karamazov* as "he who takes your soul and will and makes them his." As they wandered in ragged clothes, forsaking the world, the *startsy* experienced more freedom than others. Most were older, saintly men. Rasputin, in spite of his following, was considered a fake by many. He was known for being dirty, with filthy hair, and it was said that he smelled "like a goat.". Still, when he arrived in St. Petersburg in 1905, he was accepted by high ranking churchmen and through them, by two grand duchesses, who became his link to the czarina. Many courtiers who knew him recalled his bright, piercing eyes. He had a hypnotic effect, chillingly described by some who experienced it, including two prime ministers.

It was, of course, as a soothsayer and holy servant of God that Rasputin presented himself at the Imperial Palace in 1905, although he did it in a manner that somewhat startled the czar and czarina. He came dressed in his crude country boots and caftan, dirty hair and unpleasant odor, and from the start, he was strangely at ease with the royal couple. He greeted them like old country cousins; in no time at all, it seemed, he was addressing them as *Batiushka* and *Matushka*, the Mother and Father of the Russian peasants, and kissing them casually whenever they met. Both of them were deeply impressed with Rasputin's hypnotic eyes and air of mysterious self-assurance, as if he knew some unique secret and was on easy terms with supernatural forces. This man seemed to them to be a wonderful example of the great, inarticulate mass of Russian peasants who were their subjects, yet with whom they had never managed to establish any communication or connection.

"The czar needed a peasant," said one of Nicholas's head courtiers, and the czarina needed one too. She knew she was unpopular with the Russian upper classes, but she cherished the romantic notion that the millions of obscure Russian peasants were lovingly loyal to her and the czar. Rasputin's supernatural air reinforced Alexandra's idea that he was typical of the people, for she devoutly believed that, in their untutored faith, the simple people of Russia were more directly in touch with God than the ordained priests of the Orthodox Church.

Rasputin soon showed what he could do for young Alexis, the heir-apparent to the throne. He would sit at the bedside of the czarevich and in direct, colorful peasant language tell enchanting stories of Siberia. When Alexis had a headache, it needed only Rasputin's hand on his brow to make it go away; or sometimes the prophet just spoke to the boy on the telephone, telling him the headache would disappear, which it promptly did. What was far more important, Rasputin demonstrated on several occasions that he could stop the bleeding when the young prince fell or ran into something. How this was done was a total mystery to the doctors called in by the czar. The effect has often been explained as a psychosomatic cure. The boy's faith in Rasputin's power was so strong that once the *starets* had convinced him the bleeding would stop, it really did stop. More recent research, though, suggests that hypnosis could have this effect, through its relaxation of the blood vessels.

To the czarina, it was the miracle she had been praying for, incontestable proof that "our Friend" (as she and Nicholas called Rasputin) had been "sent to us by God." Pleasantly surprised at the shower of good effects arising from the favoritism of the royal family, Rasputin set up a comfortable establishment in St. Petersburg. Soon rumors of high living and low pleasures began to filter back to the palace. It was all just spite, Alexandra believed, which true saints often had to endure. In her letters to the czar, she often referred to Rasputin as "Him," and in some sense she considered him to be divine, a kind of reincarnation of Christ. To others, he was seen as debauched, especially as his reputation for seducing all manner of women and girls increased. His hypnotic effect by all accounts extended to the bedroom.

By 1912, Rasputin was beginning to be an important political figure. His intimacy with the royal family was now well known, and because of it, many people who wanted favors or information, or who hoped to influence the czar in his decisions, fawned upon Rasputin. Although he did not seem to be personally greedy - except where good food, good wine, and pretty women were concerned - he accepted gifts readily enough, sometimes immediately giving the money away to poor people without even counting it. In return, he would scribble a note in his bad handwriting - he had little education - to demand a favor of some official. Usually, all the note said was: "My dear friend, do it - Grigori," and that was enough. By now, he was dressing in silk blouses, sometimes embroidered by the czarina, suede breeches, and patent leather boots, but still using his peasant's cloak. It was not reported whether he bathed.

The combination of his growing political power and his notorious sexual habits was to make Rasputin a leading topic of discussion in the Fourth Duma, was elected in 1912. On the whole, the membership in that Duma was conservative; but conservative or liberal, the spectacle of the bearded peasant living in luxury and enjoying first claim on the attention of the czar and czarina was more than most upper-class Russians could stand. Moreover, opponents of the regime found in Rasputin's sinister influence a powerful argument to use against the autocracy. Nasty rumors began circulating about the nature of Rasputin's friendship with the czarina. These almost certainly unfounded tales intensified the dislike that many members of the nobility felt for "the German," as she was often called. Meanwhile, the hierarchy of the Orthodox Church was split between those who denounced Rasputin as a creature of the Devil and those who supported him rather than incur the displeasure of the czar and czarina.

Around the time of the March revolution in 1905, while Lenin was still in Europe, another radical figure emerged in Russia, someone from the same part of the country but with a different notion of revolution. They would in time be rivals. In another irony, Alexander Kerensky also was the son of an education director, a school headmaster, and grew up in a privileged household. It wasn't until he went to university in St. Petersburg that he became interested in politics. In fact, like many Russians, he had been a supporter of the czar and wept copious tears when Alexander III died. During this time, higher education had become more available and was quite inexpensive. Even sons and daughters of peasants could attend.

Caught up in the swirl of student politics, with its waves of agitation, including mass meetings and strikes, Kerensky favored the Narodniki or People's Party. To him, the Marxists were a European movement while the People's Party was home grown and more to his Russian ideals. He became a political lawyer and traveled all over Russia defending political prisoners. In time, the Marxists, led by Lenin, would fight to overthrow the czar and establish a communist government while Kerensky took a more conservative view.

At the time of the March rebellion, Kerensky was a Duma member. He acted as the communicating link between the provisional government and the Soviet.

Kerensky came from the provincial town of Simbirsk, on the Volga River, where he was born in 1881. His father was the headmaster of the two local high schools, and this led to one of the curiosities of Russian revolutionary history. For Lenin was also born in Simbirsk and it was Kerensky's father who wrote the glowing recommendation of his star pupil. Lenin was about eleven years older than young Alexander, so they were never in school together; yet to Kerensky it always seemed strange that two boys who had "breathed the same air . . . heard the same peasant songs and played in the same college playground" should have taken such different paths to the Russian Revolution and ended as bitter enemies.

Of the two, Kerensky was by far the more typical of the thousands of young Russian intellectuals who, despite their upper-class background, were forced by conscience to struggle against the autocracy of the czars. When he was eighteen, he left his father's comfortable home and went to St. Petersburg to enroll in the university. Although controlled by the government, universities were nevertheless the most active centers of revolutionary thought. "We became the enemies of the Autocracy," Kerensky wrote later, "almost as soon as we entered."

Kerensky studied law, and shortly after he graduated in 1904, he began thinking of devoting his life to the cause of Russian freedom. This soon got him into trouble. As one of a small group putting out a revolutionary weekly called *The Storm-Finch*, he came to the attention of the czarist police. Just before Christmas 1905, he was picked up for possession of inflammatory leaflets, and he spent four months in solitary confinement. Like most revolutionaries, he regarded this as a badge of honor, and he put the time to good use working out in his mind how he might best use his talents to further the cause when he got out. Normally, a young lawyer's easiest course was to become a civil servant, but Kerensky did not want to be a cog in the machine of government. Instead, he decided to specialize in defending people charged with political crimes, and he soon proved to be a skillful practitioner.

In 1912, Kerensky was one of three political lawyers appointed by members of the outgoing Third Duma to investigate an ugly incident at some gold mines in Siberia. There had been a police massacre just as brutal as that of the 1905 Bloody Sunday. About 200 people, including both workers and their wives and children, had been machine-gunned to death. The work of the investigating commission brought Kerensky much favorable attention, and that same year, he was elected as a member of the Fourth Duma. He was a Socialist Revolutionary, but the socialist parties had been outlawed. He entered the Duma as a representative of the Trudoviks, or Group of Toil, a small labor faction formed for that election.

By 1913, Rasputin and the Duma were thus, figuratively speaking, face to face. On the side of the autocracy, the czar had allowed his reactionary advisors to push him into an attitude of rigid antagonism toward the Duma; Rasputin and the czarina urged him to dissolve it altogether, or at least deprive it of all its real powers. On the side of reform stood the Duma, where Kerensky was one of the most radical leaders. He was an eloquent public speaker. He always impressed people with the fiery intensity of his conviction that Russia must throw off the chains of autocracy and adopt a more liberal form of government.

The opposition between throne and Duma was heightened when, in 1913, the 300th anniversary of the Romanov dynasty was magnificently celebrated and the importance of the Duma in the ceremonies was deliberately slighted. There was an exciting moment in the great Kazan Cathedral when Rasputin insolently sat himself down in one of the seats that had been set aside for the Duma.

M. V. Rodzianko, President of the Duma, grabbed the "man of God" by his tunic and bodily threw him out of the church despite Rasputin's effort to outstare him with his glittering eyes. In Kerensky's opinion, the *starets* was "like a living symbol of the decline of czarism."

As the year 1914 opened, even the more conservative members of the Duma were continually criticizing the czar, his Council of Ministers, and Rasputin. The chronic dissatisfaction was reflected in the working class by a great increase in the number of labor strikes. The secret police predicted the outbreak of a mass revolution.

Then, in the summer of 1914, something even bigger broke out: World War I.

4
THE CZAR AT WAR

World War I was the first great war in which the soldiers of the chief nations involved wore steel helmets, and the "till hat" became almost a symbol of that war. Russia, however, was an exception: Its millions of soldiers went to battle in visored, cloth caps that gave no protection against bullets or flying shrapnel.

The Russian soldier's jaunty cap suggests much about Russia's role in the war. In spite of recent strides toward industrialization, Russia was still basically an agricultural country. Most of its troops were peasants who had been drafted from remote farming communities. In weapons, equipment, and transport, its army had been only slightly modernized since the lessons of the

Russo-Japanese War in 1904-05. The valor of the Russian infantryman was Russia's best weapon; but in the end, it turned out to be no match for Germany's heavy artillery, masses of equipment, and the stubborn, systematic fighting of its steel-helmeted soldiers.

At the start, in the summer of 1914, it looked as if the pressure of the war effort against Germany might overcome the crosscurrents of discontent and disunity that rocked the Russian ship of state. On June 28, the heir to the throne of Austria-Hungary was assassinated in the provincial town of Sarajevo. The plot was traced to the small neighboring country of Serbia, which Russia was pledged to defend. Austria then made demands that threatened Serbia's independence, and Germany stood behind Austria. Thus it was that by the beginning of August 1914, Russia reluctantly found itself confronting war with both Germany and Austria. Although not alone, Russia's powerful friends, France and England, were far away.

The Russian people, most of whom heartily disliked everything German, rallied enthusiastically behind the czar's government. Worker strikes came to an end. Bolsheviks were rounded up and jailed. The Duma dissolved itself. There were shows of patriotism against anything German, including its embassy, shops, and offices. Soon after the declaration of war, the name of the imperial capital was changed from the German-sounding St. Petersburg to the more acceptable Russian name, Petrograd. The patriotic excitement seemed to overwhelm nearly everyone. Yet the peasant soldiers sent to fight the war had little notion of why they were fighting. Rasputin, who was in his Siberian village recovering from a stab wound given him by an angry woman, sent an ominous telegram to the imperial palace: "Let Papa [the czar] not plan war; for with war will come the end of Russia and yourselves, and you will lose to the last man."

In France and England, it was hoped that Russia's enormous army would smash into Germany by sheer force of numbers, and people spoke optimistically of "the Russian steam roller." The figure of speech was not a good one, for the Russian army was unable to maintain any momentum. At the front, everything depended on men and horses; there were no tanks and comparatively few airplanes; there were hardly any motor trucks and practically no roads solid enough for them to use anyway. Russian field artillery, though excellent in quality, fired relatively small shells, which always seemed to be in short supply. Bringing up matériel and reinforcements from the rear was a task that fell almost entirely on the Russian railroad system. It soon proved to be hopelessly inadequate.

Nevertheless, with a gallantry that aroused the admiration even of the German generals opposing them, the Russians struck hard against Germany and Austria in the summer of 1914. In the north, they invaded East Prussia with much success at first, for the Germans at this early stage of the war were concentrating on France. In the south, Russian armies attacked the Austrian province of Galicia with equally good luck. Germany, however, rushed reinforcements to both fronts by means of its excellent railroads, and by the end of 1914, the Russians had been stopped, and in some places, heavily thrown back.

Their losses were appalling. The German artillery dumped thousands of tons of high-explosive shells on the Russian infantry, slaughtering them by whole battalions. Sometimes the czar's soldiers did not even get a glimpse of their enemy. Ammunition supplies became disastrously low; many a Russian regiment attacked without artillery support. With only a few rounds of cartridges for their rifles, the men had to depend on their bayonets. Some of the units were short of rifles; soldiers often had to go without until they could pick up the weapons of fallen comrades. The war was proving to be larger, longer, and far more devastating than anyone could have forecast. Unlike its enemies and allies, Russia was not able to increase production of war goods enough to meet the demands of a prolonged conflict.

Before the war was a year old, prospects for a Russian victory were dim. Nearly 4 million Russian soldiers had been lost: killed, wounded, or taken prisoner. There were not nearly enough doctors or field hospitals, which meant that thousands upon thousands of untended wounded men suffered horribly. "The regular army," wrote a top Russian general, "had vanished." Replacements more often than not were half-trained peasants who barely knew how to fire a rifle.

At this critical point, Nicholas decided that what the Russian armies needed was to have their czar on active duty at the front, leading them in battle for the glory of Mother Russia. It was a foolish notion. Nicholas had no practical experience as a military commander and only the haziest concepts of military strategy and tactics. But it appealed strongly to his romantic and patriotic nature.

The czar's decision to go a-soldiering could not have been worse for war-torn Russia, and it was vehemently opposed by nearly all his ministers and advisors. But the little emperor who could sometimes be so easily swayed could also be very obstinate about something close to his heart. On September 2, 1915, he presided over a meeting of the Council of Ministers at the Imperial Palace. Almost desperately, the ministers argued that his going to the front would amount to a kind of abdication; that is, it would in effect leave the Russian throne vacant at the seat of the government. Nicholas listened with a show of his usual politeness, holding clenched in his hand a religious icon, a small picture of one of the saints. (It probably was the icon of Saint Nicholas that his wife had given him to take to military headquarters; it had been blessed by Rasputin.) When everyone had finished speaking, he got up and said simply, "I have heard what you say, but I adhere to my decision." A day later, he left for the front.

There is no doubt that both Rasputin and the czarina encouraged the czar to take command of the armies despite the advice of his ministers. Alexandra was jealous of the Grand Duke Nicholas Nikolayevich, the commander-in-chief, a man who towered nearly a foot above her husband and who was very popular with the Russian soldiers. This was bad enough, she thought, but in addition, the Grand Duke showed no respect whatever for her favorite holy man. Rasputin had proposed a trip to headquarters so that he could personally hang up an icon there, to which the Grand Duke is reported to have replied by telegraph: "Come and *I'll* hang you."

Rasputin had naturally been affronted by the Grand Duke's snub, yet he realized that with the czar away at the front for long periods, he would be able to exert even more influence over the czarina. To counter the opposition against him from members of the Duma, he would convince Alexandra to persuade her husband to appoint Rasputin's friends as ministers.

In one of the most astonishing episodes of modern times, a badly informed and superstitious empress sabotaged the government of a great empire by constantly nagging the emperor to make the governmental changes recommended by an ignorant Siberian peasant. This would have been crippling at any time, but under the awful strain of war, it was calamitous.

The czar's rejection of his ministers' plea that he stay at the helm of the government marked a sharp turning point in Russian history. After this decision had been made, there could be little chance of stopping the country's plunge toward revolution.

Even while Nicholas was trying to make up his mind whether to take personal command of the armed forces, evidence had been mounting from all sides that the people of Russia were ready for a last tremendous effort to work together as a unified nation under the czar. But it was necessary first for the czar to acknowledge the terrible pressures the war was bringing to bear upon his country by granting some fundamental reforms.

Already the leading citizens of the country, working through the Duma and through organizations set up by their local governments, had voluntarily taken into their own hands many of the war problems that ought to have been solved by the czar's government. The *zemstvos* of thirty-five Russian provinces, for instance, had combined with a national council of mayors from the larger cities and formed what was called Zemgor, the Russian Red Cross. Zemgor did much to help the struggling Russian army, providing hospitals, medical supplies, food, transportation for wounded soldiers, and many other essential services.

The critical problem of supplying enough matériel for the army, especially ammunition, also was tackled by a citizens' group, headed by M. V. Rodzianko and Alexander Guchkov. They proposed a national Defense Council for this purpose. The czar agreed that it should be established, much to the distress of the czarina, whose comprehension of warfare hardly went beyond her son's toy soldiers, and whose hatred for "that horrid Rodzianko" was growing. "Russia, thank God, is not a constitutional country," she reminded her husband. "[yet] these creatures try to play a part . . . it is a fright if one gives in." The Defense Council was approved by the Duma in August 1915, and by early 1916, it had begun to increase the flow of supplies to the army. These organizations in time created a huge infrastructure, an alternative government with little control from the monarchy. This exercise in self-government became a pillar of the revolution to come.

But although Nicholas was reasonable and cooperative about anything that had to do directly with the welfare of Russia's armed forces, he was strangely insensitive to the deep desire of his people for a better society. Any reform, he believed, would simply have to wait until war's end. "In general I don't pay attention to what they say," he had remarked blandly to his minister of war when the Duma met at the beginning of August. To a certain extent his going off to army headquarters was an expression of his disdain for dealing with the elected representatives of the people.

Ironically, the czar's departure not only aroused a joint protest from his Council of Ministers, but it also helped bring the quarrelsome political groups in the Duma into closer agreement than they had ever reached before. With the exception of the Marxists and socialists on the extreme left and the reactionary conservatives on the far right, they combined to form what was known as the Progressive Bloc. Their program, which was widely published, called above all for "a government based on the confidence of the public," pointing out that "only a strong, firm, and active government can lead the country to victory." They wanted the czar to choose a new Council of Ministers who would work in close harmony with the Duma and Zemgor and thus give Russia a government more responsive to the will of the people.

But it was not to be. Hardly had Nicholas reached his headquarters at the front (actually, Mogilev was a comfortable place a safe distance behind the lines) when he began to receive a torrent of letters from Alexandra. She wrote every day, pouring out everything pell-mell in her rather offbeat English: details of her health; the children's doings; who had come to tea; the latest words of wisdom from Rasputin; and last, but not least, her conferences with the old prime minister, I. L. Goremykin, who came to consult with her often.

It was through this ancient gentleman, who had been prime minister back in the days of the First Duma and who had now returned to office, that the czarina kept track of what was going on in the Fourth Duma and in the Council of Ministers. In her very first letter to Nicholas after he left for headquarters, she showed her intention of keeping her hand, guided by Rasputin, firmly on the government:

"Do not fear for what remains behind . . . Lovy, I am here, don't laugh at silly old wify, but she has 'trousers' on unseen, & I can get the old man [Goremykin] to come & keep him up to be energetic . . . It is all much deeper than appears to the eye . . . you showing your mastery, proving yourself the Autocrat without which Russia cannot exist . . . God is with you & our Friend for you. All is well . . . Sleep well my Sunshine, Russia's Saviour."

And in the same letter, she began to badger him to get rid of the minister of the interior, whom she despised, and appoint in his place a man named Alexis Khvostov, whose only apparent qualification for the job was that Rasputin was on good terms with him. Before long, she was to succeed in winning this appointment and Khvostov turned out to be typical of most of the men Alexandra and Rasputin managed to put into powerful positions: rotten through and through.

Before that happened, however, Goremykin went to headquarters in mid-September 1915, to discuss with the czar the demands of the Progressive Bloc, or rather, since he fully shared the opinions of the czarina about the Duma, to warn his master of this new surge toward democracy. Nicholas sent him back with authority to suspend the Duma immediately.

Even the more conservative members of the Council of Ministers were indignant when the suspension was announced. After Rodzianko informed the Duma members that they must go back to their homes, it was all he could do to get them peacefully to leave the Duma chamber at the Tauride Palace. Petrograd's big factories staged a two-day strike to show their resentment at the government's having taken a step backward just when everyone else was eager to move ahead. On September 19, Zemgor chose delegates to go to the czar's headquarters and express its feeling that the Duma must be quickly called together again. Nicholas flatly refused to see the delegation. It was clear that the czarina's constant demands that he be more autocratic were working.

There was a glimmer of renewed hope when the czar ordered the entire Council of Ministers to report to him at headquarters. Was it possible that he had decided, after all, to reorganize his government along the lines suggested by the Progressive Bloc? Those who hoped so would have been disturbed to know that the meeting had been planned in consultation with the czarina. She had actually advised Nicholas to prepare for the meeting by combing his hair several times with a comb given him by "our Friend," as a kind of magical protection against "those odious ministers." Instead of making any concessions, the czar rebuked them for listening to the radical proposals of the Progressive Bloc. Soon afterward, he began to replace them with more docile men recommended by Alexandra. The first was Khvostov, as minister of the interior, a post in some ways the most powerful in the empire, since it carried with it control over the secret police and censorship of publications.

The consequence of Czarina Alexandra's mismanagement of national affairs, always with Rasputin's advice, was summed up by the former commander in chief of the army, the Grand Duke Nicholas: "It is now a reign of chaos."

Petrograd was enveloped in intrigue, disillusionment, and social collapse between the fall of 1915 and the winter of 1916-17, an atmosphere that spread like a fog to every corner of the Russian Empire.

Since Rasputin was a key figure, enormous amounts of time and money were spent by those in the know in attempts to buy and use his influence with the czarina. But these attempts at intimacy with him, which included bribing, concealing his sexual exploits from Alexandra, and having him followed everywhere by secret police to protect him, were often complicated by intense jealousy of his power. Khvostov, for instance, whom the czarina had ardently supported as minister of the interior, got involved in a plan to have the "man of God" murdered. Although his plan miscarried, its discovery meant his downfall with the astonished and furious Alexandra.

Khvostov was merely one of a fairly rapid succession of ministers, most of whom were either grossly incompetent or corrupt or both. The most outstanding example was the prime minister who replaced old Goremykin: a disaster named B. V. Sturmer. This widely hated tool of Rasputin, it was hinted in Duma speeches, was no better than an agent of the German enemy. With the rapid changes of high officials, the Russian government had neither dignity nor stability. "Ministerial leap frog," one member of the Duma called it. The last minister of the interior before the revolution was perhaps the worst yet: A. D. Protopopov, a weak and foolish man believed by many who knew him to be on the edge of insanity.

The combination of such a shambles in the government and Russia's terrible defeats before the guns of Germany produced in the populace a feeling of deep and cynical disillusionment. Gone was the patriotic fervor of 1914; it was replaced by despair, a feeling of unavoidable defeat. "Getting empty in the villages," a peasant said to a British visitor; and indeed it was, as the millions of killed and maimed were followed by thousands more with every passing week. The agony of these losses was not relieved by the knowledge that the woman now guiding Russia's policies was herself of German birth. Many suspected her, unjustly, of secretly sympathizing with the enemy.

One of the worst features of the war as conducted by the Russian government was a terrible lack of coordination between the front and the rear, between what was controlled by the generals and what was controlled by civilian officials. Even the minister of war had very limited authority over the army's general staff; he was unable to override some of its most harmful policies.

The generals decided, for instance, that as the Germans relentlessly advanced into Russian territory, they would do what Russian generals had done in 1812 when Napoleon had unsuccessfully invaded Mother Russia. This was the scorched earth policy of destroying everything that might be of use to the enemy as the Russian armies retreated: burning crops, deliberately wrecking water supply systems, blowing up bridges. This, of course, made the invaded areas uninhabitable for the local Russian citizens, and several millions of them were forced to flee eastward with the few possessions they could carry. The roads were glutted with overloaded peasant carts and milling crowds of terror-stricken refugees, many of them sick and near starvation.

5
RASPUTIN'S END AND A CZAR TUMBLES

The immense stream of uprooted, desperate, suffering humanity, as described in ministerial discussions, "rolls along the roads interfering with military traffic and completely disorganizing the rear of the army . . . Men and women die by the hundred from hunger, exposure, and disease. The death rate among the children has reached a terrible height. Unburied corpses are left along the roads. The decaying carcasses of dead animals poison the atmosphere. And this flood of humanity spreads over all Russia, adds to war-time hardships, creates a shortage of foodstuffs, increases the cost of living, and accentuates the discontent which is nowhere lacking."

By the fall of 1916, the food shortage and the high cost of living had become acute problems. Actually, as one of the world's greatest agricultural countries, Russia had plenty of food. The difficulty was in moving it to where it was needed. The peasants who produced the food were not anxious to sell their produce for money that would buy almost nothing, since nearly all manufactured goods were now being consumed by the armed forces. What they did sell, or what was taken by the government, often rotted in freight cars waiting in vain for engines to pull them across Russia's overburdened railroad network.

Meanwhile, prices skyrocketed. By Christmas of 1916, fuel was so scarce and expensive in the cities that only the well-to-do could buy it. The average factory worker found himself paying three and four times as much for food and clothing as he had paid at the start of the war; even at that, people had to stand in long lines for hours every day to get into a shop to buy their skimpy share. "The mass of industrial workers are quite ready to let themselves go to the wildest excesses of a hunger riot," said a police report from October 1916.

Short of riots, the factory workers naturally expressed their frustration by strikes, which increased at an alarming rate. At the end of October, a great wave of strikes closed nearly every plant in Petrograd. When soldiers were called out to help the police drive the workers back to the factories, they shot at the police instead of at the strikers. This was an omen of things to come, even though the mutiny was quickly put down by four regiments of mounted Cossacks.

Throughout all this, the three individuals most responsible continued blindly on their way. Rasputin, knowing full well that he was surrounded by enemies, jockeyed the Council of Ministers around as best he could for his own safety. And he continued to pass his suggestions to the czarina, for transmission to the czar.

Alexandra understood nothing of the abyss toward which the empire was rushing. She never doubted that "our Friend" was inspired by a God who would not let the imperial crown fall from her husband's anointed head, and she incessantly begged Nicholas to do what their holy man desired.

And Nicholas, isolated at military headquarters, bored as much as he was distressed by the hundreds of insoluble problems pressing down upon him, retreated further and further from his responsibility. Sometimes he feebly resisted Alexandra's urgings for a short time, but in the end, he nearly always gave in again. He even managed to convince himself that his strong-willed wife would take care of everything. "You do great service to me and to our country," he wrote her in the fall of 1916; "I am so happy to think that you have found at last a worthy occupation!"

Then, on December 30, 1916, the czarina interrupted her daily letter to the czar with a startling piece of news: "Our Friend has disappeared."

Rasputin had actually been murdered. It was already too late for his removal to make much difference in the course of Russian history, and the facts about the crime are obscure. Nevertheless, the story is an illustration of the corrupt and sinister atmosphere in upper-class circles of Petrograd on the eve of the March revolution.

Rasputin was killed on the night of December 29, 1916, by some Russian aristocrats who had lured him to the basement of a Petrograd family mansion, or palace. His body, shot, stabbed, and brutally beaten, was found by the police: It had been bound and dropped into the Neva River. Although the assassins at first loudly denied their guilt, they soon realized they would be considered heroes for having done away with the *starets*. Moreover, they felt certain that they would not be severely punished since one of them was a grand duke, another a prince married to a niece of the czar's, and a third a prominent member of the Imperial Duma. Before long, they were boasting about the murder to their friends.

The motive for killing Rasputin is said to have been

a patriotic desire to rid Russia of an evil influence. Yet the character of the three chief conspirators (there were five in all) was hardly more admirable than that of their victim. The ringleader was Prince Felix Yusupov, twenty-nine-year-old heir of one of Imperial Russia's wealthiest families. By his own description, he was a spoiled playboy who had spent his youth carousing in Petrograd, Paris, and London. One of his favorite diversions had been to dress as an elegant woman and go out to balls and night clubs, where he drew much flattering attention from gallant army officers unaware of the disguise.

The Grand Duke Dmitri Pavlovich, one of Yusupov's closest friends, was a cousin of the czar and a favorite of the royal family. His behavior during the war years, however, disturbed the czarina very much. An officer in the horse guards, he either hung around the czar's military headquarters, doing nothing in particular, or went on long leaves to Petrograd to join Yusupov in wild parties and visits to gypsy entertainment spots.

The third principal member of the murder ring was V. M. Purishkevich, a far-right-wing Duma member known for his passionate hatred of all liberals, radicals, and Jews. He was one of the organizers of a group of reactionaries known as the Black Hundreds, who worked with the secret police in promoting anti-Jewish riots.

Aside from that, Purishkevich was noted for his witty speeches in the Duma, and sometimes, his scandalous clowning.

Having decided, according to Yusupov's later published account, that Rasputin must be assassinated, the conspirators went about it very deliberately. They decided to poison the "man of God" and a doctor friend of

Purishkevich's was called into the plot to provide potassium cyanide. Prince Yusupov had cultivated Rasputin's friendship and invited him to a private party at the palatial Yusupov family mansion on Gorokhovaia Street at midnight on December 29.

It has never been clear why Rasputin agreed to go, especially since there had already been several attempts on his life and he knew that most aristocrats hated him. Yusupov (who was still living in 1967) has told different stories at different times, one version being that Rasputin was eager to meet Yusupov's attractive young wife, Irina, the czar's niece. (Irina was actually in the Crimea in December 1916, recovering from influenza.) At any rate, Rasputin was ready and waiting at midnight when Yusupov arrived to pick him up in a motor car; he was dressed in his best clothes - a white silk blouse embroidered with cornflowers, velvet breeches, polished boots, and a raspberry-colored cord for a belt. Obviously, he expected some extraordinary entertainment.

At the Yusupov palace, elaborate preparations had been made. An unused apartment in the basement had been specially furnished as if it were a stage-set for a melodrama: Rich draperies and rugs had been installed, heavy tables and carved chairs moved in, lanterns hung, and a cozy fire built in the big granite fireplace. Why it was thought necessary to poison Rasputin in these surroundings rather than in one of the upstairs apartments of the big palace has never been explained.

Yusupov claims - and the story told by the assassins themselves is all we have to go on - that he took Rasputin into the downstairs hideaway and plied him with cakes and wine. The cakes and the glass from which the *starets* drank were heavily poisoned with potassium cyanide, enough, the doctor had promised, "to kill several men instantly." Rasputin looked somewhat ill, but otherwise, nothing happened. Amazed and frightened, Yusupov went upstairs to confer with his fellow conspirators, who had been impatiently waiting for news and whiling away the time by playing phonograph records and, apparently, drinking rather heavily.

Yusupov then went downstairs again, he says, taking with him Dmitri Pavlovich's revolver. When Rasputin was not looking, Yusupov pointed the gun at him and pulled the trigger. Rasputin gave "a wild scream" and fell heavily backward onto a bearskin rug. At the sound of the shot, the other conspirators came tumbling down the stairs, accidentally hitting the light switch and throwing the scene into momentary darkness. When the lights came on again, the doctor examined the body and declared the "man of God" to be dead. The assassins all went upstairs, congratulating each other that they had succeeded in ridding Russia of the evil man.

Yusupov says that at this point, he felt "a vague misgiving"; then "an irresistible impulse" made him go downstairs once more. To his utter horror, Rasputin's "corpse" had come back to life. It rose from the floor, "foaming at the mouth," and attacked Yusupov. "A ferocious struggle began. I realized now who Rasputin really was," Yusupov wrote later. "It was the reincarnation of Satan himself who held me in his clutches."

The fantastic tale ends with the superhuman mystic pursuing Yusupov up the stairs and bursting through a "locked" door into a snowy courtyard. Purishkevich chased him outside and felled him again with four shots from a pistol. The amateur assassins finished their job by taking Rasputin's body to a lonely bridge on the Neva River and dropping it over the side, where it broke through the ice. It was later reported that water was found in the lungs of the body, suggesting that Rasputin was still alive when he sank into the Neva.

During all these macabre goings-on, the police had

not been entirely unaware of something amiss at the Yusupov palace, and although they did not find the body for two days, they began an immediate investigation. Such was the myth of Rasputin's power that working class women swarmed to the spot where his body was found so they could dip "holy water" from the river. The czarina, not surprisingly, was horrified at the disappearance of "our Friend," and she had a definite idea of who the chief culprits were. On December 31, 1916, she telegraphed the czar at his military headquarters: "I fear that these two wretched boys [Yusupov and the Grand Duke Dmitri] have committed a frightful crime . . . Start today, I need you terribly."

Rasputin had prophesied that his death would bring doom to the royal family: "So long as I live, the imperial family will also live; when I die, they will also perish." It was to be a year and a half before that prophecy was fulfilled. But there can be no doubt that the murder of the notorious *starets* added to Russia's unsettled state at the end of 1916. The attitude of most peasants, for instance, probably was well expressed by a soldier who said to a government official, "Yes, only one muzhik [peasant] ever got through to the czar, and him the masters killed."

As for the czar and the czarina, they did not change their ways after Rasputin's death. As if in vengeance, they went ahead with more bad appointments of stupid and ignorant ministers. The explosive resentment of the Russian people - a resentment now shared by a very broad cross-section that included many members of the nobility as well as peasants, soldiers, and workers - could not be contained much longer. The year 1917 opened with many rumors of plots on the part of highly placed aristocrats to assassinate the czar.

None of the plots of the distraught nobility came to anything; they were too disorganized. But the long-suffering common people, without quite realizing it themselves, were about to act. Their effort was to go down in history as the March Revolution.

The unexpected insurrection of March 1917, ended with the national power of Russia in the hands of two rather antagonistic groups. The Executive Committee of the Soviet of Workers' and Soldiers' Deputies was dominated by socialists, with a minority of Bolsheviks. The provisional government represented the moderates, some liberal and some conservative, of the old Duma. One man was a member of both bodies. Alexander Kerensky, minister of justice in the provisional government and vice chairman of the Petrograd Soviet, had the hard task of maintaining a link between the two groups and preventing them from working at cross-purposes.

Initially, it looked as if all might go well. The Soviet Executive Committee decided that it was best to let the provisional government take the lead, while it stood by as a kind of watchdog of the Revolution. This fitted in with left-wing political theory, which assumed that a bourgeois, democratic republic would be necessary as a transition between czarism and socialism or communism.

There was a basic flaw in this assumption - one that both the Soviet's radical socialist leaders and the moderate liberals of the provisional government like Kerensky failed to see at first. A democratic republic could function only with the support of broad masses of the people. The public would have to understand the sometimes slow and careful methods by which a representative democracy solves its problems. They would have to understand that liberty implies tolerance for many differing views.

The Russian people sadly lacked experience with democracy. Moreover, the enormous impact of the war, which had hastened the collapse of the outworn system of the autocracy, had left the country in a state of painful disorganization and discontent. The great masses of ordinary Russian citizens were in no mood for delay, especially in solutions to the two problems that seemed to plague their very existence: the continuation of the war and the failure to get more land into the hands of the peasant farmers. They thought these matters should be taken care of quickly, and they felt more and more that if the Revolution meant anything, it meant just that.

The provisional government, unfortunately, took a different view. The attitude of Kerensky was typical. Looking as he did toward the Western European democracies as models for the government he hoped to see in Russia, he felt that Russia's military obligations to England and France were binding. Russia must fight on against Germany, despite its appalling losses, despite the desperate state of its economy, despite the plunging morale of its troops. As for the redistribution of land to the peasants, Kerensky felt that it must wait until a Constituent Assembly, scheduled for the fall of 1917, could meet and set up a democratic system for deciding such matters.

Meanwhile, in the first happy flush of the new revolutionary era, the provisional government tried to introduce all at once a set of fundamental liberties such as Russian reformers had dreamed of for generations. There would be freedom of speech and of the press; legal equality for everyone; voting privileges for everyone; complete freedom of political activity. In keeping with these reforms, men who had been jailed or exiled to Siberia for political reasons were immediately released; those who were in foreign countries for their own safety were allowed to return.

The new freedom was especially meaningful to the Bolsheviks, who had been forced to operate mostly under cover. Now the Bolshevik leaders began to come back to Petrograd like homing pigeons suddenly let out of their cages.

The supreme Bolshevik leader, however, found it impossible to rush straight home. In Switzerland, Lenin had been watching the revolutionary developments in Russia with surprise and pleasure. But Germany, with whom Russia was still at war, stood between him and his native land. How could he get back to Russia?

He got there, as it turned out, with the help of the German government. The Germans knew that Lenin would be no more inclined to support the provisional government, largely made up of capitalist liberals, than he had been to support the czar. They also knew that one of Lenin's Ten Commandments of Bolshevism, so to speak, was that the Russian people had no reason for fighting Germany and ought to pull their nation out of the war as soon as possible. During 1916, Germany had suffered huge losses against the Allies on the Western Front, and by early 1917, it was apparent that the United States would soon declare war and send over millions of troops. A separate peace with Russia was something the kaiser hoped for very much; with the Eastern Front eliminated, he still might be able to win the war.

Toward the middle of April 1917, a train carrying about thirty Russian exiles, with Lenin at their head, made its way through Germany to the Baltic Sea.

German military authorities allowed its transit on condition that none of its passengers be allowed out to spread their infectious revolutionary theories in Germany. When the sealed train reached the Baltic, the travelers were hastily embarked for Sweden, and from there, they crossed through Finland into Russia. It was the first time Lenin had come home in ten years.

The Bolshevik chief got what can only be called a mixed reception. Members of the provisional government knew he was the prince of troublemakers and hostile to their attempts to build Russia into a constitutional democracy, but they knew also that his return with the help of the enemy, Germany, would bring charges of treason against him. They decided to leave him alone, hoping that the Mensheviks and Socialist Revolutionaries, who outvoted the Bolsheviks in the Soviet Executive Committee, would keep him subdued.

The Soviet leaders, however, did not quite know how to treat Lenin. He was acknowledged to be one of the great chiefs among socialist politicians, yet it seemed that he had gotten out of touch with reality during his long exile from Russia. They had entered into a working agreement with the provisional government, including a policy of limited support to the war effort, but Lenin had given no hint that he was ready to make practical compromises. Just the same, some official notice had to be taken of his arrival, and Nikolai S. Chkheidze, the Menshevik chairman of the Petrograd Soviet, went to the city's Finland Station on April 16 to greet him.

At the station, the Bolsheviks, with the cooperation of several contingents of soldiers, sailors, and workers who were sympathetic to them, had arranged a colorful welcome. Banners with revolutionary slogans were hanging everywhere; red and gold triumphal arches had been set up; a military band blared out the Marseillaise and other appropriate tunes. The train was late, and the excitement of the crowd grew. When the returning hero finally arrived and walked into the station, Chkheidze made a short and rather embarrassing speech in which he welcomed Lenin but expressed the hope that he would not work toward any disunity that would injure the Revolution.

Lenin paid no attention to Chkheidze. Instead, he greeted the workers, soldiers, and sailors as "Dear comrades" and as "the advance guard of the international proletarian army," winding up with: "Long live the worldwide socialist revolution!" That brought a great cheer from the crowd, and outside the station, Lenin was enthusiastically hoisted to the hood of an armored car, where he made another speech denouncing war. Then, with dusk falling and the vehicle's headlights cutting through Petrograd's evening gloom, the welcoming procession began to move slowly across the city. Every now and then it would stop long enough for Lenin to clamber to the top of the armored car and make his speech over again to the people who surged around the intersections, cheering and singing. Even though the whole affair had undoubtedly been planned carefully by the Bolsheviks, it was impressive to everyone who saw it.

What the Bolsheviks had not planned was the way Lenin spoke to them when he attended a reception given by the party leaders that evening. It was as if a football team who imagined they were doing pretty well in a big game were given a half-time tongue-lashing by a coach who told them that, on the contrary, they were about to lose the game. Lenin denounced the Soviet Executive Committee for compromising with the provisional government. He insisted that overthrow of the bourgeois government could be the only possible goal for the Bolsheviks. Then Russia could make a separate peace with Germany and begin building a communist society. "We don't need any parliamentary republic!" he shouted. "We don't need any bourgeois democracy! We don't need any government except the Soviet of workers', soldiers', and farmhands' deputies!"

The stunned Bolshevik leaders soon found that Lenin meant exactly what he said. His program of militant revolution, the so-called April Theses, was published in the pages of the Bolshevik newspaper, *Pravda,* one of whose chief editors at this time was Stalin.

6
CHAOS AMID WAR AND REVOLUTION

D espite opposition even from members of his own party, Lenin had history on his side in the spring of 1917. Under the guidance of Prince Georgi E. Lvov, the provisional government's prime minister, the measures taken to meet actual conditions were not very effective. The cost of living continued to mount steadily, and the factory workers grumbled bitterly; no vigorous steps were taken to help the peasants toward their desire for more land; the war dragged on with no prospect of an early peace. In May, Professor P. N. Milyukov, the Kadet leader serving as foreign minister in the provisional government, assured the Allies that Russia would go on fighting Germany till the bitter end. Mass demonstrations protesting Milyukov's pledge broke out in the streets of the capital, coming close to bloodshed.

Things did not go much better even after Milyukov resigned, which he did shortly. Guchkov, the former Octobrist who was Prince Lvov's minister of war, resigned at about the same time. After heated debate, the Soviet Executive Committee decided to participate in a coalition with the provisional government. Five more socialists joined Kerensky, who became minister of war, in the reorganized cabinet. The Bolsheviks remained aloof, heeding Lenin's slogan: "All power to the Soviets; no support to the provisional government." At the First All-Russian Congress of Soviets, held at Petrograd in mid-June, a moderate socialist complained that there was no party in Russia ready to take power. "Yes, there is," shouted Lenin from his seat.

Kerensky, meanwhile, announced his intention to push the war against Germany with renewed vigor. Morale in the army had never been lower, as proved by mass desertions, and in some episodes, flat refusals to fight. Yet Kerensky recommended a new offensive against the Austrian sector of the enemy line. The entry of the United States into World War I had encouraged nearly all political elements in the hope that this powerful new ally would somehow enable Russia to defeat Germany. The new minister of war toured the front, making eloquent speeches to arouse the soldiers. His offensive began early in

July and soon turned into a serious retreat, not for the Austrians and the Germans who helped them, but for the Russians.

Passionate antiwar feelings erupted into new disturbances in Petrograd when the losses in Kerensky's offensive were published. It is not quite clear even today whether those riotous events, which became known as the July Days, were actually planned by the Bolshevik headquarters or just quietly encouraged by them. At any rate, the whole thing backfired, from their point of view. Gangs of soldiers and sailors roamed the streets, shooting more or less haphazardly at ordinary citizens and killing or wounding some 400. The government called in troops from outside the capital to put down these disorders, and after a few days of terror, the city quieted down. The moderate Kadets left the government; Prince Lvov resigned, and Kerensky became prime minister.

Whether the Bolsheviks had really been responsible for the July Days or not, it was widely reported that they had been. The provisional government, by now disillusioned with the idea of complete political freedom, attacked the Bolsheviks fiercely, accusing them of being pro-German. *Pravda* was shut down, and orders were issued for the arrest of Lenin and his chief lieutenants, Lev Borisovich Kamenev and Grigori E. Zinoviev. Only Kamenev was caught; Lenin and Zinoviev quickly went into hiding, and in September, they escaped across the border into Finland. From then until October 22, the Bolshevik chief had to command the operations of his party by long-distance communication, mostly by letters sent to subordinates such as Stalin, who were still free in Petrograd even though under close observation by the government.

More important than Stalin, at this stage, was the Menshevik leader Leon Trotsky, who had come back to Russia from the United States in May. He was ready to join forces with Lenin's Bolsheviks for an overthrow of the middle-class government whenever the time should appear ripe. Claiming to be just as subversive as Lenin, Trotsky arrogantly demanded that the provisional government arrest him, too. When he was released in mid-September, he helped the Bolsheviks win a majority vote in the Petrograd Soviet and soon was elected president of that body.

By late summer of 1917, the overall situation in Russia was as chaotic as it had been a year earlier, when the czar still ruled. There were endless official and unofficial discussions about what ought to be done: meetings, conferences, congresses, some called by the government, some by the Soviet, some by the various political parties. The most impressive gathering, the Moscow State Congress of late August, brought together 2,400 delegates from all the country's "live forces" - former Duma members, trade unionists, bankers, municipal representatives, and members of various soviets. The Congress soon split into irreconcilable right and left wings, with Kerensky at the center, unable to achieve unity.

The millions of words earnestly spoken in Russia that summer did little to change the realities of the war, the collapsing economy of the country, and the dark mood of most of the soldiers, workers, and peasants. In the provinces, bands of furious peasants drove landlords from their estates and burned their manor houses. In the army, thousands mutinied, while thousands more deserted. Peasant soldiers returning from the war came home with new skills and abilities. In addition to learning to handle weapons, they had learned to organize, had become more literate, and had finally realized how long they had been exploited in wars waged by the rich. They would soon become soldiers in the revolution.

Without the slightest understanding of the works of Karl Marx, the great masses of the Russian people were gradually drifting into a state of mind that was susceptible to the Bolshevik program of total overthrow of the existing system. The workers' revolution was born in the bread lines, where workers exchanged the latest gossip, rumors, ideas, and anger. Since their situation could hardly get much worse, why not discard what they had and start over, especially if it meant the end of the hated war.

On the other hand, there were those who thought that Russia's real troubles had started when the monarchy fell. Some looked back wistfully to Nicholas II, who was now in exile with his family at Tobolsk, Siberia; others felt that although the czarist days were gone forever, a right-wing, conservative government might restore some of the old glory.

One of those with strong conservative views was General L. G. Kornilov, whom Kerensky had made commander-in-chief of Russia's armies. Kornilov demanded suppression of the Bolsheviks and other radical elements and hinted that if the provisional government could not accomplish this goal, he would. Rumors of a military *coup d'état* reached Petrograd, and Kerensky promptly dismissed Kornilov. The commander-in-chief replied by ordering a picked force under General A. M. Krymov to move toward Petrograd.

Kerensky, for all his brilliance, was now on the horns of a dilemma that was too difficult for him. He knew that the mood of the people, in general, was moving further and further to the left - that is, toward the program that Lenin and his Bolshevik followers kept declaring could be won only by the violent overthrow of the provisional government. But to allow Kornilov and his right-wing followers to overthrow the government instead would mean a counterrevolutionary reaction that might even restore the monarchy and bring the ex-czar back from Siberia. Although he remained unsympathetic toward the Marxists, Kerensky was even less sympathetic toward the reactionaries. In desperation, he turned to the Soviet.

The Soviet leaders, including SRs and Mensheviks as well as Bolsheviks, immediately took vigorous steps to upset Kornilov's counterrevolutionary plans. The Petrograd garrison got ready to fight; the factory workers were issued rifles; barricades were built across the main avenues leading into the city. Several thousand army officers in Petrograd who were suspected of being sympathetic to the Kornilov plan were suddenly arrested. But all this proved unnecessary, for the Soviet's almost total control over the railroad system was an even more powerful weapon. The troops dispatched by Kornilov under General Krymov found themselves derailed onto sidings or left standing in their cars while the locomotives pulling them were detached and taken elsewhere. Soviet leaders then dissuaded the soldiers from marching into the city and firing upon their "brothers." It all ended with the arrest of Komilov, while the disgraced General Krymov, shot himself.

The most important result of the Kornilov fiasco was that it gave the Bolsheviks a chance to come out of hiding under the banner of "stop the counterrevolution." Lenin still remained cautiously in Finland, but Trotsky was on the scene in Petrograd, diligently working for the proletarian uprising that both of the Bolshevik leaders were now convinced was inevitable in the near future if they played their cards right.

They did play them right. On October 23, a resolution calling for a definite insurrection was adopted at a Bolshevik meeting. Lenin was present at the meeting, having secretly returned from Finland the day before, his beard shaved off and an odd-looking wig on his bald head to further the disguise. Three days later, the Petrograd Soviet set up a Military Revolutionary Committee, supposedly to organize the defenses of the capital against possible German attack. Dominated by the Bolsheviks, the committee instead acted to alert the Petrograd garrison of the new insurrection, warning the soldiers to be ready to take arms against the Kerensky government in order to save the Revolution.

Time was now growing short, for on November 7, the Second All-Russian Congress of Soviets, with delegates from all over the country, was to meet in Petrograd. Lenin and Trotsky were determined to present the Congress with the Bolshevik insurrection as an accomplished fact since they feared the Bolshevik delegates would be in a minority. This was no time, they reasoned, for democratic procedures: They would seize power first and justify it afterward. Besides, they both believed that, in a sense, a Bolshevik revolution would be truly democratic since it would aim to give the Russian people what they wanted: bread, peace, and land.

By the night of November 6, 1917, the Bolshevik camp was highly organized. Not only did Lenin and Trotsky have the promised support of most of the Petrograd garrison of troops, but in every big factory, a unit of workers' militia - later famous as the Red Guard - was more or less trained, more or less armed with illegal rifles, and more or less ready to carry out specific duties in the insurrection. Special units had been designated to take over the telephone exchange, the railroad stations, the state bank, the printing plants, and the drawbridges spanning the Neva River. Whether each unit would carry out its revolutionary duty remained to be seen; but in any case, Trotsky, who did most of the planning, had thought of just about everything. Nothing could have made a more telling contrast with the March revolution, which had occurred haphazardly, without any planning whatsoever.

Nor could there have been a sharper contrast with the March revolution when the Bolsheviks' plans were actually put into effect, beginning about 2:00 a.m. on November 7. Instead of tumultuous street fighting, all went quietly, with ridiculous ease. In later years, when it was necessary for the sake of Soviet mythology to make the Bolshevik revolution sound as heroic as possible, stories of sharp encounters in the night, of fierce battles at particular buildings, and of daring exploits by individual insurrectionists were invented. In reality, there was little of this sort of dramatic revolutionary activity at the time.

It was not that Kerensky's government had been unaware of the Bolsheviks' plan. The insurrection had been openly discussed for days before it took place, and even the timing was well known. As a matter of fact, on November 5, in its meeting rooms at the Winter Palace, the government issued a number of anti-Bolshevik decrees: Their papers were to be shut down; the Military Revolutionary Committee was to be arrested; the Smolny Institute (a former school for girls where the Soviet now met) was to be cut out of the city telephone system; troops were to be called in from outside the city. The only trouble, as Trotsky ironically observed, was that "in these formidable orders it was not indicated who was to carry them out or how."

There really was almost nobody to carry them out. The most reliable troops the government had on hand were the recently recruited Women's Battalion and the young cadets of the various military schools in Petrograd. Many of these valiantly tried to resist the Bolshevik rebellion, but with few exceptions, they were ineffective. They were hopelessly outnumbered and hopelessly inexperienced.

By nightfall on November 7, a date sacred to communism, nearly all of the city of Petrograd was in the hands of Bolshevik-led forces. There had been hardly any bloodletting at all, and some citizens were not even aware that a revolution was taking place. The streetcars continued to run as usual; most restaurants and shops were open for business; people even went to the opera and theater as if everything were normal.

Meanwhile, at the Smolny Institute, the members of the Petrograd Soviet, almost crowded out now by the arriving delegates to the All-Russian Congress of Soviets, were behaving as if talk were the essence of revolution. The brightly lit building swarmed like an anthill. Outside in the courtyard, dozens of autos and armored cars stood waiting, many with motors running as if impatient to be off to the scene of the action. Inside, the Bolshevik top command alternated between giving out bulletins on the latest successes of their forces throughout the city and arguing loudly with Mensheviks and Socialist Revolutionaries.

It was not until eleven o'clock on the night of November 7 that the Congress finally got under way. It was more of the same: talk, talk, talk. But before long, the opponents of the Bolsheviks began to realize that all the talk would get them nowhere: events were passing them by. Most of them walked out of the Congress. At about 2:30 a.m., the chairman announced that the last stronghold of the Kerensky government, the Winter Palace, had fallen to the siege of Bolshevik soldiers and workers. After three more hours of excited talk, the delegates, dead tired, voted in favor of a resolution stating that the Congress of Soviets would take over governmental power in Russia. Then everyone who had a bed to go to went to it, gratefully.

The "siege" of the Winter Palace, though it was the closest thing to a battle during the insurrection of November 7-8, had been something of a farce. Inside its ornate halls, the ministers of the Kerensky government were protected by about 200 military cadets, nervous members of the Women's Battalion, many stacks of rifles, and an enormous supply of fine wines that had been stored in the cellars in czarist times. Kerensky himself, seeking reliable troops, had hastily departed from the city that morning, escorted by an automobile borrowed from the American embassy and flying the American flag. After unsuccessful attempts to rally Russian troops in his support, Kerensky returned in disguise to Petrograd. When the Bolsheviks ordered his arrest, he traveled to England and survived to become one of the most famous of Russian exiles. In 1967, at the age of eighty-six, he was still vigorous and living in New York City.

The Bolshevik forces surrounding the Winter Palace on the night of November 7-8 were formidable. On the Neva, the cruiser *Aurora*, whose sailors had come over to the new revolution almost to a man, was occasionally firing its heavy guns at the building. The guns were loaded with blanks to avoid destroying the palace unless necessary. Machine-gun detachments and infantry companies were strategically placed around all sides of the Winter Palace, and it looked as if only outright surrender would prevent a massacre if and when the Bolshevik forces attacked.

7
BOLSHEVIK VICTORIES AT A COST

Central Petrograd, on the night of November 7, 1917, was the stage setting for a drama that changed forever the history of the great Russian empire and of the entire world. That night saw the overthrow of the provisional government by the Bolsheviks and the establishment of the first communist state.

Eventually, it was discovered that some of the doors to the building had been left unguarded, and a number of Bolsheviks entered through them, wandering around the many corridors and halls, accosting the defenders and trying to argue them into surrender. In the end, the forces outside did rush the palace in a frontal attack, but by then, the situation was so confused that, although there was much excitement, only six attackers were killed. There were no casualties among the defenders. The ministers of the Kerensky government were placed under arrest and taken off to the Fortress of Saints Peter and Paul; and the Petrograd phase of the revolution - the most important - was over. Moscow Bolsheviks timed their uprising to coincide with that of their Petrograd comrades, but bloody fighting raged in the ancient capital for a week, with a good deal of damage to historic buildings of the Kremlin. By that time, however, local soviets had wrested control of most other Russian cities from the provisional government.

The great event in Petrograd was ratified, in a manner of speaking, at the second session of the All-Russian Congress of Soviets, on the night of November 8. Lenin now appeared in the open, without his wig, and addressed the Congress. John Reed, an American reporter who was there, described the scene:

A thundering wave of cheers announced the entrance of the presidium [the elected leaders of the Congress], with Lenin, the great Lenin, among them. A short, stocky figure, with a big head set down on his shoulders, bald and bulging little eyes, a snubbish nose, wide, generous mouth, and heavy chin; clean-shaven now, but already beginning to bristle with the well-known beard of his past and future . . . Now Lenin, gripping the edge of the reading stand, letting his little winking eyes travel over the crowd as he stood there waiting, apparently oblivious to the long-rolling ovation, which lasted several minutes. When it finished, he said simply, "We shall now proceed to construct the Socialist order." Again that overwhelming human roar.

On that night of November 8, constructing the socialist order began with a vote to issue proclamations on three basic questions: the war, the land, and the form of the new government. There were long discussions and debates - the session did not end until five o'clock in the morning - but Trotsky later pithily summed up what the proclamations said on those three questions: "end the war, give the land to the people, establish a socialist dictatorship." That, for the moment, expressed the Bolshevik program, and even though many of the delegates to the Congress were not Bolsheviks, they apparently all were moved by this sweeping directness. At one point, everybody stood and sang a funeral anthem, in memory of those who had fallen in the war. N. N. Sukhanov, there as an observer, remembered later: "The whole presidium, headed by Lenin, was standing up and singing, with excited, exalted faces and blazing eyes . . . the delegates were completely revived . . . The masses were permeated by the faith that all would go well."

The faith of the masses was going to be sorely tested during the coming months and years. Constructing the socialist order with acts rather than proclamations would prove to be a very difficult matter.

"The day will come," the British statesman Sir Winston Churchill declared in 1953, "when it will be recognized without doubt throughout the civilized world that the strangling of Bolshevism at birth would have been an untold blessing to the human race."

Some strenuous efforts were made between 1918 and 1920 to do just that, but for the moment, conditions were far from encouraging, and it sometimes seemed a historical miracle that Russian communism survived and grew. Its success can be attributed partly to luck, partly to the bungling of its enemies, and partly to sheer guts and brilliant improvising on the part of the Bolshevik leaders, especially Lenin.

Lenin, although he had an unquenchable inner flame of Marxist conviction, was above all a realist and a man of action. He said that starting the Communist Revolution in Russia was "as easy as lifting a feather"; he knew only too well that to keep the Revolution alive would be more like moving a mountain. To do this, he was prepared to take any necessary steps, including self-contradiction, deliberate lies, suppression of civil liberties, forced labor, and coldblooded killing.

Judged by the standards of right and wrong that most Americans believe in, the Bolshevik takeover of the Russian Revolution was an evil event. But Marxist standards of right and wrong rest on different assumptions.

Marxism does not accept the idea of God. Since there is no God, the Marxist argues, there is no God-given set of moral laws or commandments that men and governments ought to obey. (After the communists had made belief in Marxism one of the requirements for any public office, and even for getting into a Russian university, this joke was popular in Moscow: A student is asked by a professor, "What is God?" "God," says the student, "is a mistaken idea of the capitalistic class; there is no God." "Very good," says the professor; "you pass." "Thank God." the student exclaims.)

In the Marxist view, laws and customs are merely a reflection of the desires and interests of the ruling class. In a capitalist society, for instance, they reflect the desires and interests of the property owners, nothing more. On the other hand, the Marxist believes in determinism - that is, he believes that all events, past and future, are rigidly determined by laws of cause and effect that operate just as certainly in social relationships as they do in physics, chemistry, or biology. And just as biological evolution goes through a definite series of phases from lower forms of life to higher, so human society goes through a series of evolutionary phases. Essentially, for the Marxist, the evolutionary stages of society are feudalism (such as prevailed in Europe during the Middle Ages), capitalism (the stage of individual ownership), and communism. Communism, since it is the highest form, is the system toward which all human society inevitably moves.

This belief goes far to explain certain characteristics of communists that often baffle non-communists. It throws light on their stubborn, even fanatical insistence that in the end, communism is bound to triumph and nothing can stop it. It also helps explain how a communist can coolly commit what non-communists consider to be terrible crimes. He believes he is simply an instrument through which irresistible historical forces express themselves and anything he does to help advance communism is, therefore, self-justified. Yet even though it is supposed to rest on scientific grounds, there is no way of proving that this belief in the inevitability of communism is valid. It really is a matter of faith, in a sense a Marxist substitute for religion.

The Marxist theory of determinism, however, has another peculiar feature. The theory insists - again without any genuine scientific support - that human nature is fundamentally molded by the kind of economic system under which people happen to live. If they are factory owners under a capitalist system, for instance, they will have a set of beliefs and values that are quite different from those of the proletariat, or working class. By the same reasoning, in a communist society, where the capitalist class has been eliminated and only the proletariat remains, everyone will have basically the same values and attitudes.

From the democratic point of view, this theory of economic determinism is the fatal flaw of Marxism, for it leads to a deadly conclusion: In a truly communistic world, there could be no real conflict between the government and the people, for the government would *automatically* express the people's values. Individual freedom would, therefore, be meaningless. As a matter of fact, in some rather hazily distant future, communist theory sees a utopian time of super democracy, when there will be no need for government in the ordinary sense. The people, all workers who jointly own all the material wealth of the world, will simply run things more or less instinctively, happily agreeing on everything of importance. This was what Lenin meant by a phrase he made famous, "The withering away of the state." "While there is a state," Lenin declared, "there is no freedom. When there is freedom, there will be no state."

There would have to be a transitional period, of course, and it was this period that Lenin and his fellow Bolsheviks believed they were entering after their success on November 7. During the transition, however long it might take, Russia would be ruled by what the Bolsheviks called the dictatorship of the proletariat. In theory, this meant that the masses of toilers - the peasants, fishermen, miners, factory workers - would collectively act as a dictator in order to stamp out capitalism and resist any counterrevolutionary individuals or groups, whether inside or outside the country. In practice, since the masses were in an extremely unsettled condition, it meant that the local and regional soviets would run the country as directed by the All-Russian Congress of Soviets. The Central Executive Committee of the Congress, in turn, delegated actual governmental authority to the Council of People's Commissars, or Sovnarkom, as it was often called. Thus the power really flowed from the top of the pyramid down, even though in principle the people were the source of all power. Whatever Sovnarkom and the Bolshevik leaders decided to do, they could claim that their actions represented the will of the people. This kind of thinking was used to justify a rigid censorship over all newspapers and books as part of the dictatorship of the proletariat.

Although he never lost his interest in theory, Lenin was much more concerned about practice during the tense and dangerous months following the Bolshevik *coup d'état*. He concentrated especially on three problems. First, if he and his group were to keep their hold on the government, they must see to it that their opponents have no power. At the same time, the Bolshevik leadership had to rally most of the Russian people to support them. Third, the threat of the German army still hung over the country and something had to be done quickly about that danger.

The political problem arose immediately, for a national election called by the Kerensky government was still slated for November 25. Its purpose was to choose delegates to a Constituent Assembly, which would debate the question of just what kind of society the new Russia ought to have. Inevitably, the delegates would also debate whether or not to approve the Bolshevik government. The Bolsheviks dared not call off the election, which they knew had tremendous popular appeal; yet, just as they feared, they came out very much the underdogs when the votes were counted. Out of 707 delegates, only 175 were Bolsheviks. Leading the poll were the Socialist Revolutionaries, with over 400 delegates. Only about forty of the SRs were far enough to the left in their views to be considered allies of the Bolsheviks.

In this embarrassing situation, Lenin caught his opponents off balance by agreeing to let a few Left SRs into Sovnarkom, thus forming a coalition government. When the Constituent Assembly met, on January 18, 1918, however, the Bolsheviks closed it down after a few hours. Outvoted, the Bolsheviks and Left SRs walked out of the Tauride Palace, where the Assembly was meeting. The armed guards the Bolsheviks had stationed at the palace then announced they were "tired" and hustled the remaining delegates out of the building. Crowds gathered in Petrograd to protest the dissolution of the Assembly, but Bolshevik troops scattered them with rifle volleys. It was as harsh a suppression as any the czar had ever used against the Duma. The Bolsheviks justified their action by arguing that the suppression was for the people, not against them. The Constituent Assembly, they said, had been chosen on a basis that did not truly represent the proletarian masses and the peasants of Russia.

Despite these highhanded tactics, Lenin proved he was nimble when it came to rallying the greater part of the Russian people behind the new government. Marxist theory called for putting all the land immediately under national control. Instead, Lenin announced a policy whereby any peasant family had a right to the land they worked themselves and to the crops they harvested. Only the great landowners were to have their land taken away from them. The Bolshevik leaders also understood that if factories were to continue production without serious interruption, they would have to do so largely under the supervision of the owners and managers of the old capitalist regime. Therefore, they left most of the factories as they were for the time being, although committees of workers were to be chosen in each plant to supervise production. In other words, the communist program was to be introduced gradually. Lenin was always ready to compromise, at least temporarily, when he felt that it was in the Bolshevik interest to do so.

As for the war with Germany, the Bolshevik government was in no position to do anything except compromise. Although he had to convince most of his colleagues, including Trotsky, Lenin insisted that an immediate peace treaty was necessary if the Bolshevik government was going to survive and begin to put its program into operation. A preliminary armistice with Germany had been signed in mid-December 1917, and peace negotiations opened toward the end of that month. After several weeks of bickering with the Central Powers, the Bolshevik delegation, headed by Trotsky, announced that it would not sign a peace treaty. Nor, Trotsky said to his astonished adversaries, would Russia continue to make war. The nation would simply withdraw from the front and demobilize its forces. The Germans promptly began a new advance against Russia on February 18, 1918, and were met with practically no resistance from Russian forces. It was obvious they could push on to Petrograd and Moscow virtually unopposed. Under that threat, the Bolsheviks unhappily signed a peace treaty at Brest-Litovsk, Poland, on March 3. The harsh treaty deprived Russia of huge chunks of territory (including Finland, Estonia, Latvia, Lithuania, Poland, and the Ukraine) and about one-third of its population. Moreover, Russia lost one-third of its farmlands, one-half of its industries, and up to 90 percent of such important resources as coal. What the Bolsheviks got in return was a chance to strengthen their control inside the territory left to them, without fear of German invasion.

Russia's new leaders had plenty of other worries. The Left SRs resigned from the government in protest against the treaty, but they continued to agitate against the Bolsheviks, sometimes only with words but sometimes with plots.

In the summer of 1917, after some months of comfortable confinement at Tsarskoe Selo, Nicholas II and his family were removed to Tobolsk, Siberia. The Bolsheviks, taking over in November, provided rougher guards and less food for the captives, and in April 1918, moved them to Ekaterinburg in the Urals. As anti-Bolsheviks moved westward, it seemed that the family might be freed and Nicholas restored to power. On July 16, however, Bolshevik guards took the family to a basement room on a pretense of moving them somewhere else. The czarina noticed there were no chairs; three were brought for her, the czar and their son. The girls stood behind them. As they waited, a firing squad entered the room and began shooting.

Diamonds sewn into the women's clothing blocked some of the bullets, so the guards finished them off by bayonetting them. All were killed, their bodies thrown into a mineshaft. There was now no chance of Nicholas returning to the throne.

The vast empire that Nicholas lost in March 1917, and that Kerensky, in turn, lost to the Bolsheviks the following November, was besieged on all sides by mid-1918. Under terms of the Treaty of Brest-Litovsk, the communists had been forced to surrender to German occupation forces the heavily populated areas of Poland and the Ukraine. In vain attempts to keep Russia fighting against Germany by toppling the Bolsheviks, the World War I Allies landed forces in North Russia and Siberia during the summer of 1918. Earlier that year, the Czech Legion had controlled much of the vital Trans-Siberian Railroad. Through 1919, White leaders (anti-Bolshevik, anti-Communist), such as A. I. Denikin, A. V. Kolchak, and N. N. Yudenich, pressed the Bolsheviks from every side - the first nearly taking the new capital of Moscow, the latter almost seizing Petrograd.

The spring and summer of 1918 were an exceptionally difficult period, Trotsky wrote later. "At moments there was the feeling that everything was slipping and crumbling . . . The question arose whether there was in the exhausted, ruined, desperate country enough sap to support the new regime ... Everywhere conspiracies were festering."

To combat conspiracies, the Bolsheviks set up a secret police organization, called Cheka (an abbreviation of its Russian title), which soon proved to be just as fierce and possibly more efficient than any such organization under the czars. It was one of the ironies of the Russian Revolution that the man who directed the hundreds upon hundreds of executions without trial carried out by Cheka was F. E. Dzerzhinski, a Marxist idealist who formerly had spent much of his energy organizing relief for homeless and neglected children. Now he was like another person. "Counterrevolutionaries, spies, speculators, ruffians, hooligans, saboteurs and other parasites," he announced, "*will be mercilessly shot by [Cheka's] detachments on the spot of the offense.*" This was the beginning of what came to be known as the Red Terror, and it had Lenin's full support as a necessary defense of the Revolution. "There has never been a single revolution and period of civil war without executions," he declared.

Meanwhile, the economic condition of Russia was rapidly deteriorating. Czarist mismanagement and the terrible strains of the war had left the nation in bad shape at the time of the March revolution in the winter of 1917. The fumbling efforts of the provisional government under Kerensky had not improved matters. Now the Bolsheviks were in power, but Lenin's careful plans to avoid depressing economic activity by too rapid an application of communist principles were not enough to keep matters from growing still worse. By June 1918, food supplies in the cities were frighteningly low; it was clear that many thousands of peasants must be hoarding their grain because they got so little in return for it. Factory production was also at a new low. Some of the government leaders were convinced that Lenin's reluctance to push ahead with nationalization of agriculture and industry was the cause of Soviet Russia's economic troubles. Now they got their chance to try to prove it.

A new policy, which came to be known as War Communism, decreed that all big factories would be taken over by the government, and along with this, all workers were subject to labor conscription - that is, they had to work where, when, and at what the government directed. To solve the food shortage, a "food army" was established, and contingents of armed men roamed the countryside, taking grain from the peasants by force when necessary. In March 1918, the Bolshevik leaders had moved the capital from Petrograd, with all its czarist memories, to Russia's ancient capital of Moscow. About that time, they also changed their official name to the Communist Party. Comparing the initial joy of the November revolution with the hardships that soon followed, confused peasants began complaining that the generous Bolsheviks had given them land, but the cruel communists were taking away from them the food they had grown on their new property.

In the long run, War Communism was not very successful and was eventually given up. It was unable to meet the emergency situation that had led to its introduction and for which it was named: civil war. Before the Bolsheviks came to power, about 45,000 Czechoslovak soldiers, most of them deserters from the Austrian army, had been formed into a corps to fight with Russia against Germany. After the Treaty of Brest-Litovsk took Russia out of the war, the Allies hatched a scheme to take the Czech troops around the world to fight Germany on the Western Front. Trainloads of Czechs were sent along the great Trans-Siberian Railroad toward the Pacific port of Vladivostok. But the transit of so many foreign troops across Russian soil created tension, and a number of violent clashes broke out between the Czechs and local soviets. This led to a general uprising of the Czech troops, and by June 1918, they were in control of several important parts of Siberia, as well as sections of the middle Volga River and Ural Mountain regions. Anti-Bolshevik Russians swarmed to their banner, and soon the government in Moscow realized that the tired Bolshevik forces would have to be revitalized to fight off this new threat. Trotsky, as War Commissar, took charge of the Red Army and immediately began to demonstrate surprising genius as a military organizer and leader. Nevertheless, he was obliged to draft his soldiers instead of relying on volunteers as he originally had hoped to do.

To add to Trotsky's troubles, the Allies decided to intervene in Russia. They were naturally very unhappy that their German foe was no longer fighting on two fronts and hoped to revive the Eastern Front. Some Allied leaders argued that intervention was necessary to end the civil war by crushing the Bolsheviks and restoring a strong government that would continue fighting on their side. Early in August, a small British force landed at the northern port of Archangel, on the White Sea. The weak Bolshevik forces there hastily withdrew southward, with the British in pursuit. In early September, the British were joined by 5,000 American troops, who had gone to Europe expecting to fight against Germany but now found themselves off on an adventure against the communists that few of them understood. President Woodrow Wilson had dispatched the Americans with the understanding they would be used only to guard military stores the Allies had sent to Russia. They were put under the command of British generals, however, and with a good deal of encouragement from David R. Francis, the American ambassador to Russia, the British sent the doughboys straight off to the fighting front.

The Americans were in northern Russia through the winter of 1918-19, and during that time, they were the mainstay of the small Allied force opposing the Bolsheviks there. They were poorly equipped against the ferocious northern winter - temperatures often went to thirty below zero, or lower - and British efforts to use them against the communist regime came to very little. Nevertheless, some hard-fought encounters took place between American and Bolshevik troops, with a considerable number of casualties on both sides, thus poisoning the United States relations with Russia's new regime for years to come. Meanwhile, the Japanese landed forces at Vladivostok in the summer of 1918, and the British, French, and Americans soon joined them in Siberia - more to prevent the Japanese from grabbing too much territory from Russia than to suppress the Bolsheviks.

From other directions, the communist regime faced more serious threats. The Czech forces quickly pushed westward, driving the Red troops before them. Ex-admiral of the czarist Navy, A. V. Kolchak, took command of some large forces in Siberia, including remnants of the Czech corps, and launched a drive toward the Volga in March 1919. In Estonia, General N. N. Yudenich gathered another White army of about 20,000 and came near to capturing Petrograd in the fall of 1919. In the south, a large Cossack army under General A. I. Denikin continued to assault the Reds until the end of 1919, at one time driving within 200 miles of Moscow. For a while, it looked as if Denikin might succeed in overwhelming the Red armies opposing him, link up with anti-Bolshevik forces in Siberia, and overthrow the communists.

The Whites got much moral and material help from England, France, and the United States, who had forced Germany to sign an armistice ending World War I on November 11, 1918. Many Allied leaders (like Churchill) would have been extremely pleased to see the Bolshevik regime collapse. Yet none of the White armies managed to mount the final offensive that was needed to overcome Trotsky's Reds. The Bolsheviks did have two great advantages, even though they were sorely beset: They were at the center of the struggle, with shorter communication and supply lines; and they were defending the soil of Mother Russia against foreign invaders who did not pretend to match the claim of the communists that this soil now belonged, quite literally, to the Russian people.

One by one, the White leaders were defeated. They failed to form a unified front against the Bolsheviks, and enough Allied support for their cause never materialized. By the end of 1920, the civil war was over, and most of the foreign interventionists had withdrawn. The communist leaders were free to face their many other difficulties without the fear that a military disaster might smash all their hopes and plans. The Russian Soviet Federated Socialist Republic, as it was by then called, had turned out to be a tough infant despite what appeared to be the serious birth defects of the world's first communist state.

When the Soviet government had managed to survive both the civil war with the White forces and the harassments of foreign intervention, it could be said that the Russian Revolution was over. But although the revolution itself was over, the future of communism was still uncertain.

Russia was still in desperate economic trouble in 1920, but Lenin was bubbling with optimism. He thought circumstances looked promising for one of the great Marxist dreams: that the proletarian revolution would soon become worldwide. At a meeting of international revolutionaries in Moscow in July 1920 - the Second Congress of the Communist International, as it was called - he outlined a system of tightly organized communist parties in all western countries, in order to prepare for the world revolution. Only a year later, however, he was far less optimistic, for a severe economic depression had discouraged the working class in most countries. Typically, Lenin's reaction was to urge harder work by communist organizers, so as to be ready when the right time came.

Meanwhile, he had to face some painful problems in Soviet Russia itself. The iron rule of communism, especially when it went along with empty stomachs and miserable living conditions, had not produced a happy people. Just how unhappy many of them were was shockingly suggested in March 1921, when thousands of sailors at the great Kronstadt naval base, on the Baltic, openly rebelled against communist authority. These men were no reactionaries. On the contrary, they had been among the most enthusiastic supporters of the new regime, and Trotsky once called them "the pride and ornament of the Revolution." Now they were grimly disillusioned by the way the workers and peasants had been treated under the dictatorship of the proletariat and they demanded more freedom: free elections, free speech, freedom of the press, free trade unions, and freedom of the peasants to harvest their land for their own benefit.

But Lenin, Trotsky, Stalin, and the other communist leaders had no intention of allowing a new challenge to their power. In the Soviet press, they denounced the Kronstadt demands as counterrevolutionary. Then Trotsky moved 60,000 Red Army troops to Kronstadt, and in a bloody attack lasting several days, overpowered the rebellious sailors. Thousands were killed in the fighting; hundreds more were executed later.

Ever the realist, Lenin recognized that the Kronstadt rebellion was a sign of the dissatisfaction of the Russian people. In an effort to improve their living conditions and avoid further rebellions, he introduced his so-called New Economic Policy. Actually, the NEP was a retreat from War Communism to a system of economic production much more like that of modern capitalism. There was to be a good deal of private enterprise. Workers were to be paid on the basis of their productivity; peasants were to be allowed to keep surpluses and use them in exchange for manufactured goods. Private enterprises were allowed to coexist with socialized industries, and government control of the latter was relaxed. These measures succeeded fairly well in pulling Soviet society out of the economic swamp into which it had been sinking, even though a terrible famine struck the country in 1921 and 1922.

By this time, Lenin was in bad health, although he was only in his early fifties. He had been seriously wounded by an assassination attempt in 1918 and further weakened by years of strenuous activity as the leader of the Communist Party and the Soviet nation. In his modest apartment and offices in Moscow's Kremlin, he habitually worked sixteen hours a day, with excursions only to make speeches at public rallies, attend long committee meetings, or visit some new communist factory or work project. The first of three paralytic strokes hit him in May 1922, and from then on, he was a fading figure in the Soviet government.

It appears that in the few months left to him, Lenin spent much of his time reviewing in his mind the whole history of the Russian Revolution. He was concerned especially with the vision of an ideal communistic society that had moved him from the days of his youth. Only now did his elastic optimism lose its bounce: As his last writings indicate, he began to wonder whether the Soviet triumph had not, in fact, betrayed that vision by replacing the czarist autocracy with a huge bureaucracy that was equally suppressive of the interests of the common people. Far from withering away, the government had steadily grown more ponderous, extending its totalitarian control over every aspect of the life of the individual.

Moreover, Lenin was bothered by the fact that among the other Bolshevik leaders, he saw no one who struck him as having the ability to push toward the goals of the Revolution without, perhaps, making things worse instead of better. In Joseph Stalin, who seemed eager to inherit Lenin's mantle, he saw a man whose thirst for personal power was so great that it might threaten the whole future of communism. In his last testament, Lenin urged his followers to consider a means of removing Stalin from the important post he already held, that of General Secretary of the Communist Party. "Comrade Stalin . . . has concentrated in his own hands unbounded power," he warned, "and I am not sure whether he will always know how to use this power cautiously enough."

But Lenin died on January 21, 1924, and Stalin showed that he was too crafty and too firmly entrenched to be dislodged by anyone. Instead, he sooner or later got rid of most of his old Bolshevik friends and rivals – Kamenev, Trotsky, Zinoviev, and many others - by means of exile, "purge" trials and executions, or assassination. For the next three decades, the fate of the Soviet nation would rest largely in the hands of this man, who was more ruthlessly bent than Lenin had ever been to industrialize and modernize Russia, regardless of the cost in lives and freedom.

During his lifetime, Lenin had always carefully avoided allowing any cult of hero worship to grow up around him; but in death, he was unable to prevent it. Hundreds of thousands of Russians attended his elaborate funeral in Moscow. Afterward, his body, skillfully embalmed, was placed on display like a religious relic in a granite mausoleum in the capital's vast Red Square. There it lies today, visited almost constantly by long lines of faithful communist pilgrims and tourists. Under the protective glass, the well-known face appears thoughtful, as if Lenin were still pondering how the Russian Revolution could have strayed so far from his hopeful dream of a classless utopia.

Made in the USA
Las Vegas, NV
27 December 2020